A PRACTICAL HANDBOOK FOR EVERYONE WHO HAS A BANKING ACCOUNT.

BY

J. GEORGE KIDDY

(Author of "The Country Banker's Handbook," etc.).

LONDON ?
WATERLOW AND SONS LIMITED, LONDON WALL.
1909.

PREFACE.

SOME fifteen years ago the writer compiled, largely
from notes of correspondence passing between the
London Head Office and its branch banks, a small
volume entitled "The Country Bankers' Handbook,"
intended for the especial use and guidance of those
for whom it was principally prepared. The fact
that it has since that time had a continuous sale, and
is now in its fifth edition, emboldens the writer to hope
that the present work, which, in its turn, has also been
largely put together from notes of correspondence and
other items of business daily occurring between banks
and their customers and others, may prove of service
to the general public to whom it is addressed. It does
not pretend in any sense to be "legal" or even
"technical," except in so far as it is r´ e to translate
what may be included in those ex· sions into the
more common and easily understood r ctice of banking.
While it is the writer's earnest desire that the book may
be intelligible to the veriest novice into whose hands it
may come, he trusts that it will also be found of service to

the best informed upon such matters as the book deals with. Nor again is it the intention to give the rules and practice of any one bank in particular, but rather the methods and procedure of banks in general.

It may not be out of place here to state that yet one other object which the writer had in view was to combat to some extent the reprehensible tone of writing on banking subjects which was somewhat in vogue a few years ago, when the notes for this book were in an early stage. This fashion has long since died out, and reference to it now would be out of place were it not that one sincerely desires, by way of contrast to the manner in which "practices" and "tricks" of bankers were then discussed, to shew a truer picture of the relations between banks and their customers. Needless to say, a great deal of the stuff then written could not be taken seriously; nevertheless, one is reminded of the old adage that "when mud is thrown some must stick." No high end or useful purpose can ever be served by seeking to bring into conflict those who have such vital and interdependent relations as bankers and their customers. It is hoped, therefore, that the following pages will bring out in some way the vast interests that are served for customers and the general public, the frequently gratuitous and onerous services which are performed, with the many risks and responsibilities undertaken, by those who faithfully fulfil the calling of a banker.

Just a brief word may be offered by way of explanation of the title. There are others that would possibly have been more appropriate, and less suggestive of a work of fiction. It may, however, be said that such titles as "Banker and Customer" have had the changes fairly rung upon them, and it can at any rate be claimed that the one selected has the merit of bringing the personal element into prominent relief.

J. GEO. KIDDY.

FINCHLEY,
London, N.,
April, 1909.

INTRODUCTION.

THE object of this book is to render assistance to the various classes of customers of a bank as well as to those members of the community who, while they feel that they have nothing special to learn upon general matters connected with banking, would nevertheless be glad of guidance in some of its specialities, such as how to conduct Stock Exchange transactions through a banker; the various points to be remembered in reclaiming Income Tax; how to set about obtaining a Power of Attorney when going abroad; how to keep a proper record of investments; and so forth.

The author has endeavoured to keep before him the fact that a bank's customers are made up almost entirely of the undermentioned classes :—

SHOPKEEPERS ;	PROFESSIONAL MEN
FARMERS ;	OF EVERY KIND ;
MERCHANTS ;	LADIES ;
MANUFACTURERS ;	PRIVATE COMPANIES ;
FINANCIERS ;	PUBLIC COMPANIES ;

AND CORPORATE BODIES.

It is scarcely necessary to add that a bank manager needs to be a widely experienced and tactful man if he is to transact business successfully for and with such varied classes. In fact, it may be said that there is hardly a matter connected with money or credit in its various forms, at home or abroad, in which the customer requires his assistance, that the banker cannot undertake and carry through.

It may not be out of place, in these introductory remarks, to sketch in outline the various departments into which a large London bank is divided, especially if it is the head office of a country or Metropolitan (or both) institution. Some of these departments are, of course, entirely, or almost entirely, concerned with the internal working of the bank, but they are, nevertheless, of the highest importance to its proper conduct and success. Such, for example, are the Inspector's Office (or, as it is sometimes called, the General Manager's Department), the Accountant's Office and the Clearing Department. Those, however, in which the public are directly interested, the various functions of which are dealt with in

the succeeding chapters, may be enumerated
as follows :—

CASHIERS (OR TELLERS) AND LEDGER
KEEPERS ;
STOCK DEPARTMENT ;
COUPON AND DIVIDEND DEPARTMENT ;
SECURITIES AND LOAN DEPARTMENT ;
DISCOUNT OFFICE ;
SECRETARY'S OFFICE ;
CORRESPONDENCE DEPARTMENT ;
COUNTRY DEPARTMENT.

These are, of course, grouped differently in
different banks, but in the main the above
classification probably holds good for all the
large City banks.

Now an important point to be remembered
is that, while in the smaller institutions there
may be no sub-divisions such as those above
mentioned, yet precisely the same operations,
though on a much smaller scale, pass through
the hands of the three or four men in a
provincial or suburban bank as employ the
possibly thirty or forty times that number
who are spread over the various departments,
enumerated above, in a London bank. Hence
it follows that what we are about to consider

in the succeeding pages will be of equal service and application, whether the reader's "own particular" bank or branch bank is a large or small institution. The "little" institution is but a miniature of the larger one. In this connection, too, it may be mentioned that the term "head office," where used in this book, means the London Head Office, and includes "London Agent" where the country bank has no head office of its own in London.

It is sincerely hoped that this work will be found of especial value by ladies, who form no inconsiderable proportion of a bank's customers and shareholders, and to whom the mysteries of current accounts, collection of coupons, payment of dividends, investments, and many another section of banking practice are an intricate and thorny pathway. While one may be amused, one can to some extent understand, and sympathise with, the action of the lady who on being informed that her account was overdrawn wrote expressing her regret at the occurrence, and enclosed her cheque to repay the overdraft. Such an one is, however, very far removed from that small class existing on the books of every bank—a class which might be called wilfully " balance blind "—who appear to be unable to distinguish between the debit and credit side of their pass book whenever the balance is on the adverse side.

Incidentally it may be mentioned that, within recent years, many banks have undertaken the duties of trustees and executors; while two of the leading banks have opened foreign exchange departments. Probably both these movements will be adopted by other banks in the course of time.

In conclusion, we shall not be far wrong when we say that the stability and durability of any bank will always depend, in a very large measure, upon the character and capacity of those who shape its policy and to whom its course and conduct are entrusted.

CONTENTS.

CHAPTER I.—*ACCOUNTS.*

CHAPTER II.—*BILLS AND LOANS.*

CHAPTER III.—*BANK OF ENGLAND.*

CHAPTER IV.—*INVESTMENTS, ETC.*

CHAPTER V.—*DIVIDENDS, ETC.*

CHAPTER VI.—*MISCELLANEOUS.*

CHAPTER I.

ACCOUNTS.

CHAPTER I.—SECTION I.

CURRENT ACCOUNTS.
DEPOSIT ACCOUNTS.
DEPOSIT RECEIPTS.

IF you are about to open an account with a bank, either in the country or in London, the first requisite will be a satisfactory introduction. This having been obtained you will arrange with your bank manager as to the amount to be kept as a minimum balance; and the signature book having been duly signed by you and the first deposit made to the credit of your account, you will receive a cheque book, a pay-in slip book, and a pass book. Cheque books are of varying sizes, the smallest usually containing twelve cheques. For public companies, etc., arrangements are frequently made with bankers for special cheque forms to be printed, bearing the name of such company corporation, etc., prominently on the cheque. When an account is opened in the name of a

company the bank will require production of
the Memorandum and Articles of Association,
together with the Certificate of Incorporation
(if a limited company); and a mandate form,
or forms, will require to be executed, stating by
whom cheques are to be signed, securities
withdrawn, etc.

One point you will require to bear in mind
is that where the balance of your account falls
short of the stipulated minimum you will be
liable to a nominal charge at the end of the
half-year. There are some customers whose
accounts are frequently below the minimum
balance, or who sometimes issue cheques which
overdraw their accounts. The banker of course
has to be guided by what he knows as to the
respectability, character and means of the
person who thus overdraws. In a large number
of cases, he will be perfectly safe in paying the
cheques; and he would probably send a reminder
to the customer that by such payment his
account has been overdrawn by so much.

On the other hand, there *are* customers
for whom the banker, anxious to save their
credit, pays their cheques although there is
an insufficient balance to meet them; and
the amount, though small, thus placed on the

debit side of the account is never refunded, in spite of numerous reminders (the amount is probably too small to sue for); eventually such debit balances have to be charged to the banker's fund for losses. Those who have wide notions on the subject of unclaimed balances with bankers should remember that there is another side to the picture.

But of course the vast majority of accounts on the bank's ledgers work smoothly enough, and in many cases neither banker nor customer ever see each other, year in, year out. Customers living at a distance call occasionally to cash cheques; others forward their cheques by post with a request that banknotes may be sent them in exchange; cheques, bills, etc., are remitted by the customer to the bank by post for his credit: in fact a large number of a banker's customers might be classed as " postal customers." It may, perhaps, be as well to remind these in particular of a point that ought to be remembered by everyone who has a banking account, viz., that it is very desirable that the pass book should be lodged with the banker every now and again to be made up, and should invariably be sent in a few days before the close of each half-year. Of course, with large firms and public companies, who have a great number of transactions passing through their account, it is much better to send in the pass book day by day, or at least every two or three days. An ordinary account holder, however, who has, say, half a dozen to twenty entries passing through his account in the course of a month, should send in his pass book at any rate once every month or six weeks. Where pass books are kept over from the end of one half-year to the end of the next before they are forwarded to be made up, it naturally adds considerably to the labour at that time of the year which is always a particularly heavy one with the banker.

Two or three small points that may be mentioned with regard to pass books are : (1) That it is always desirable to remove from the inner pockets the paid cheques and other vouchers that are sent you with the book each time that it is returned to you made up. (2) That from amongst such vouchers, most of which you will probably destroy after you have checked them with your pass book, you should carefully put aside all those relating to income tax deducted from your dividends, placing them with your claim form. (3) Should there be any irregularities in your pass book you should at once communicate with your bank manager thereon. (4) In the event of any change in your address you should at once advise the bank. Further details and instructions with regard to matters relating to the conduct of the account, etc., will be usually found in the covers of your pass book, and should be carefully read by you. You will also probably find in the same place a list of the branches of the bank. This, too, may prove serviceable, either from the business point of view, or when on a holiday. If, for instance, you are going away either to the country or to the seaside, you will be able to see whether your bank has a branch at or near such place, and to arrange accordingly through your branch manager for the payment of your cheques there ; while again, supposing your own bank has no office at the place, your branch manager will, nevertheless, be able to arrange matters for you with any other bank at or near your holiday resort. Similarly, the customer of a country bank can arrange for the payment of any special cheques in London through his banker's London agents or head office ; or, if required, instructions can be given to the London bank for the payment of customers' cheques up to a certain amount on any given day within a fixed period. In the latter case it is customary to renew such credits for six months.

Your banker will always pay any subscriptions for you, annually or otherwise, upon your giving him the customary request together with instructions to charge the payments to your account.

To return to the subject of the cheque book, great care should always be exercised in ordering a book and in keeping it in a safe place. When ordering a new book it is advisable, in a general way, to do so by means of the request form that you will have found near the end of your previous cheque book. Such form must be signed by yourself, and if sent by hand it should be through someone in whom you have perfect trust. The risks that arise, both to the customer, but more especially to the banker, through laxity in this respect, or on account of carelessness in regard to the way in which cheque books are insecurely kept or left about unguardedly, is probably greater than many people would imagine. This is not the place nor the occasion for recounting incidents of frauds and forgery that have arisen through such neglect, but one would probably be safe in saying that there are very few bankers who cannot relate some incidents of losses entailed mainly through negligence of the proper precautions with regard to keeping a cheque book. If, however, in spite of all precautions you *should* have the misfortune to lose your cheque book, or to have one or more of the cheques stolen therefrom, you should let your banker know immediately. You should also advise him if, for some cause, you have been compelled to draw a cheque on a half-sheet of paper instead of on the proper form. Such a course should never be resorted to except in the most urgent necessity, and you must not be surprised if the person to whom you issue such a cheque has some difficulty in getting it through. As a matter of fact this method of drawing cheques has been successfully used in more than one case by some forger or set of forgers, with the result that bankers are more stringent than ever in putting a stop to the issue of such irregular forms of cheques.

A word of caution may be advisable on the subject of telegrams respecting an account. It is well to bear in mind that the banker has nothing from which to authenticate the telegram that a customer may send him ; and it is very undesirable, for example, to send him a telegram asking to be informed by wire of the present amount standing to the credit of one's account.

Another point that may be mentioned here is, that one must never forward, say, for example, a cheque drawn on the Cornhill & Leadenhall Bank direct to that bank asking them to send a remittance by post in exchange. Even if the cheque be "open" such a course would be irregular, and if "crossed" to cash it would be quite out of the question. Where a person has no banking account, his proper course is to entrust any cheques he receives to some friend who has an account, or sometimes they can be cashed by local tradesmen.

When for any reason you are closing your account, you should always return any unused cheques direct to the bank manager, and he will remit you their stamp value.

It has been the practice of late years for some customers to maintain both a Current Account and a Deposit Account, the latter bearing interest at the advertised rates. When the Current Account balance becomes low it is fed from the Deposit Account; but transfers from one account to the other can only be made under the customer's instructions. Moreover, it should be noted that if a customer merely keeps a Current Account to meet sundry payments, without maintaining a proper balance, he must not expect to escape the charge that is always made under such circumstances.

There are, of course, small deposit accounts kept in cases where the depositor prefers this method to the issue of a Deposit Receipt in his favour.

If a banker is served with a garnishee order in respect of the amount standing to the credit of his customer's account, he need not, and should not, honour any cheque subsequently presented. It is immaterial whether or not the balance due to the customer exceeds the amount of the judgment debt.

No payment but a payment made by compulsion of law can discharge a garnishee from his original liability to his creditor.

If you are an executor or administrator of someone who had a banking account and also securities lodged at his or her bankers, and it is your intention that the account and securities should continue at the bank, but in your own name, write them a letter as follows, when you or your solicitors exhibit the Probate or Letters of Administration :—

" With reference to Current Account standing in your books in the name of————, of whose estate I have been appointed Executor (or Administrator), and to the securities held by you on his (or her) behalf, I shall be obliged by your transferring the balance of the said Current Account into my own name and by your holding the said securities on my account."

It may be well also here to emphasise the fact that in current accounts, as in other matters, bankers will not recognise trustees as such.

Deposit Receipts.—With many of the Colonial banks money is received on deposit for a stated period (one year or upwards) at a fixed rate of interest. With other banks, however, when money is lodged on deposit it is subject to seven days' notice of withdrawal, and no arrangement as to length of time is made, while so far as London bankers are concerned the rate of interest varies from time to time according to the fluctuations in the Bank of England rate of discount, such variations being advertised, as they occur, in the principal London papers. For such deposits a receipt is issued, and must be produced whenever it is desired to withdraw the whole or any part of the amount. Deposit receipts are not transferable.

SECTION II.

CHEQUES.

THE subject of cheques is one of considerable importance, and merits a section by itself, while at the same time attention may be called to the remarks made thereon in connection with Current Accounts. A pamphlet might indeed be written solely on the subject of endorsement of cheques, but it will suffice here to note some of the principal points to be kept in mind. As in some other matters, so with the endorsement of cheques, amusing illustrations could be furnished of "how not to do it."

Perhaps it will be best to give these points in tabular form.

(1) If a cheque is to "Bearer" it does not require endorsement; if to "Order" it must be endorsed.

(2) The Title Mr., Mrs., Miss, Rev., etc., must not form part of the endorsement.

(3) A cheque payable to the order of
Mrs. Thomas Robinson should be endorsed by the lady in her own name,
adding beneath her signature "Wife
(or Widow) of Thomas Robinson."

(4) A cheque payable to the executors of
Mary Jones, deceased, can be endorsed
by any one of such executors "For
self and co-executors of Mary Jones,
deceased."

(5) A cheque payable to the order of the
trustees of Thomas Brown, deceased,
must be endorsed by *all* the trustees
as "Trustees of Thomas Brown,
deceased."

(6) Endorse your name as it is given on
the face of the cheque, although it may
not be correctly spelled, and though one
or more of your christian names may be
omitted. You can add your usual signature below your previous endorsement.

All cheques must be written in ink, and any
alteration must be confirmed by the initials of
the person or persons drawing the cheque.
Always write the amount in words close to
the margin on the left hand side, and keep the

figures close to the " £ " sign, writing them distinctly.

It is always advisable, when sending cheques through the post, or when paying them away, to cross them with two parallel transverse lines. They can then only be paid through some bank. Where it is desired, the name of the bank can be written in the crossing, and the cheque will then be paid only through that particular bank. If, in addition to the crossing, the words "not negotiable" are added, the person who takes the cheque does so at his risk, in case of any defect in the title. Such crossing gives additional protection, however, to the drawer, and to the paying and collecting banks also if they obey the directions on the crossing. The words, "not negotiable" should not be written across the face of the cheque without the two parallel lines also being made which constitute the " crossing."

It should be clearly understood that marking a cheque "not negotiable" does not in any way interfere with its being negotiated. It simply has the effect of preventing any holder for value from improving upon the title of any previous holder who, for example, might have picked up the cheque in the street. If the

cheque had not been marked " not negotiable "
the subsequent holder could have sued the
drawer, in spite of the cheque having been
stolen or picked up by the previous holder,
provided he received the cheque in due course
without any knowledge of any defect in the
previous holder's title.

To put the matter in another form, a "not
negotiable " cheque is the only form of cheque
which the drawer can effectually stop payment
of.

When sending cheques, etc., by post to your
banker to be placed to the credit of your
account, never put them in the pocket of your
pass-book, if you should happen to be sending
the book at the same time, as they might easily
be overlooked.

In the lower left-hand corner of nearly all
cheques will now be seen one or other of the
following initials :—" T.," " M.," or " C."
These are abbreviations for the words " Town,"
" Metropolitan," and " Country " respectively,
and they indicate the three divisions into
which the London Bankers' Clearing House is
divided.   These initial letters are of immense
assistarce to those whose duty it is to sort the
cheques up into these divisions.   Here, again,

it would be interesting to enter more fully into the details as to the working of the Clearing House system, but it would be outside the scope of this handbook, and would require an ampler space than can be afforded it within these pages.

The time limit for clearing cheques (London, Provincial, Scotch or Irish) varies, of course, to some extent with the locality of the banks at which they are paid in, as also under the system of "protest" payments; and therefore, where a customer wishes to know how soon any given cheque will be cleared he should, if such information does not appear on the pay-in slip, enquire of the cashier to whom he hands the cheque for collection. Arrangement can generally be made for ascertaining by wire the fate of a cheque where it is so desired.

Where a cheque has been lost, mislaid, or stolen, or where from any other cause you require to stop it, you should immediately notify your banker, giving him, if possible, the number and date of the cheque, as well as stating the amount, and the name of payee.

One other word may be added on the subject of "crossing" a cheque—a form of crossing that is, perhaps, slowly dying out, but which,

c

nevertheless, may yet be seen—"a/c payee." There is a good deal of misunderstanding as to the value of this. The instruction, however, is one which is not recognised by the Bills of Exchange Act, and the paying bank does not know whose account was credited with the amount by the collecting bank. Practically it may be regarded simply as a cautionary notice to the collecting banker.

CHAPTER II.

BILLS AND LOANS.

BILLS OF EXCHANGE.

The Bill Department, in all large banks, is a very important one, and here again the problem of condensing into a brief space all that it is necessary to state for practical purposes is not an easy one. The Bills of Exchange Act, coupled with the principal legal cases and "points" connected with bills, would alone compose a large volume; but the purport of this work is to discuss the practical, eve⁻y-day items rather than legal questions. It is, therefore, assumed that the reader is already acquainted with the customary form of a bill or promissory note, and he should be aware that there are always six items which may be said to "make up" a bill, which should invariably be examined to make sure as to their correctness :—

(1) Stamp Duty.
(2) Endorsement.

(3) General wording, and agreement of amount expressed in words with those in figures.

(4) Date.

(5) Due date.

(6) Acceptor.

Bills may be roughly divided into two classes, namely, inland and foreign. Those drawn and payable in the United Kingdom are, of course, inland bills; while foreign bills would be those which are either drawn in this country and payable abroad, or drawn abroad and payable in this country.

It is customary with those who accept bills to make them payable at their bankers, and such bills are therefore collected in the same manner as cheques. It may be a convenience to state here the duty on inland bills of exchange. Such duty must, of course, be represented by an *ad valorem* stamp impressed on the bill, except in the case of demand drafts and those drawn at 3 days' date or sight, for which the 1d. postage stamp is available.

Any amount, on demand, 1d.
Ditto, at 3 days' date or 3 days' sight, 1d.

On Bills of any other kind and on Promissory Notes :—

> Not exceeding £ 5 ... ... 1d.
> „ 10 ... ... 2d.
> „ 25 ... ... 3d.
> „ 50 ... ... 6d.
> „ 75 ... ... 9d.
> „ 100 ... ... 1/-

and for every additional £100 or fraction of £100, 1/-

The stamp duty on bills drawn and payable abroad, but circulated in this country, is 6d. per cent.

If an inland bill is dishonoured at maturity, it is the practice, with some oanks, to hand it to a notary public, who formally presents it, and, if payment is refused, marks the face of the bill with a note of the date of presentation, etc. A bill must also be noted for non-acceptance, if drawn after sight and refused acceptance, so as to fix the date of maturity.

Foreign bills require to be protested for non-acceptance and for non-payment, so as to preserve recourse against foreign parties thereto.

Bankers and bill brokers buy bills, or, as it is frequently termed, "discount" them for their customers. The rates of discount vary from day to day, and can be ascertained by reference to the Money Market column of the leading daily papers. Naturally the rates vary according to the class of paper, and the period for which the bills have to run. In fact there are many "shades" of bills, starting from what are known as Bank Bills, and going down through the Fine Trade Bills to the documents which are more humble both in their amounts and classification. With regard to this last-named description of bill, the customer of course cannot expect to get it discounted at the fine rates quoted for the better class of bills. The bank manager, or bill broker, as the case may be, has, moreover, to take into consideration, not only the quality of the bill, but also the status of the customer who wishes it to be discounted.

Where foreign and colonial bills are sent by a country bank to its London office for sale, the bank has to endorse such bills before they can be sold, and thereby becomes liable for the amount involved, unless they are drawn under a bank credit. In some cases the banker may therefore require a covering limit, as in the case of discounts, where he receives any foreign or colonial bills for sale other than those drawn under credits.

The practice of making out bills by the aid of a typewriter is to be deprecated, as it has been found that bills so drawn lend themselves more readily to fraud than those made out by handwriting.

A great many bills lodged with bankers are only deposited for collection, and are therefore held by the banks until the date of maturity. They occasionally prove of service if a customer-wishes to overdraw his account for a sho·period.

As is only natural, the discounting of bi renders necessary an immense number of quiries with regard to the respectability standing of the acceptor, and sometime. other signatories to bills. Of course, in case of banks, large mercantile houses, many well-known companies and trading (lishments, no enquiry is necessary. As re the ordinary class of acceptor, an enq¹ made of his bankers as to whether he in the way of business for such and s amount. Not only in respect of bills, regards other matters also—for exam sponsibility as a guarantor or for the re a house—enquiries have frequently to by one bank of another. A point to in mind in this connection by the customer is, that these enquiries should a:ways be made *through his banker*, as it is contrary to banking practice to reply direct to any enquiry made by a firm or private individual.

To revert to the subject of bills sent abroad for collection—the charges made for this service by the various banks naturally varies considerably according to the part of the world ᵕ which such bills are to be collected. The ᵕarges for collecting a bill in some small town South Africa, for instance, would of course heavier than those for collecting a bill for ᵕnilar amount payable, say in Montreal or ᵕbec.

ᵕe local bill stamps also vary ; in the ᵕralasian Colonies, while the stamp duty ᵕbills of exchange "on demand" or "at ᵕ" is 1d. in most of the Colonies, and the ᵕof other stamp duties is identical for ᵕAustralia and Tasmania, there are at ᵕvo other different scales for the other ᵕᵢ.

ᵕ circulars issued by various Eastern, ᵕAfrican, Canadian, Australian, etc., ᵕhe following instructions, which have ᵕracted as being of fairly general application to most of them, should be carefully noted. Such instructions must, of course, be given to *your own* banker, who would in turn transmit them to the bank to whom he entrusted the bills for collection. They should state :—

(1) As to the disposal of documents (if any) attached to the draft. Such documents would usually consist of Invoices, Bills of Lading, and Policies of Insurance, and Consular Invoice if necessary.

(2) The rebate to be allowed, should tl̄ drawee wish to pay under discour otherwise the rate allowed will be ru by local conditions.

(3) Whether to protest in case of n acceptance $\frac{and}{or}$ non-payment.

(4) How the goods are to be disposed o case of non-acceptance $\frac{and}{or}$ non-payr and

(5) The name of an agent in case of n(

In some cases it will be necessary special clause to be embodied in the for instance, where the collection cha to be borne by the drawee, or in ord̄ the amount payable in currency.

cases, before drawing, or at any rate before completing the bill, it will be well for you to consult your own banker as to the phraseology of such clause, since it will of course vary, according to the locality on which, or the special purpose for which, the bill is drawn.

Here it may be mentioned that bills of lading, to constitute a security, should always be made out to the order of the consignor, and endorsed in blank; not to the order of the consignee, as in the event of non-acceptance of any dispute, your bankers' agents would ve no control over the goods, and could not rehouse and insure them on your behalf.

While mails are, of course, now more juent, and there are further facilities by er routes, than was the case within quite nt years, it still remains a general rule to bserved, so far as can be conveniently that all bills and documents should the London head office, or agents of vincial bank, on or before Thursday g of each week to ensure their dispatch jut-going mails for the East and for frica. If the bills, etc., can be in a day sooner, so much the better. ently American mails were made up in London on Wednesdays and Saturdays, and bills and documents for these mails were required to reach the London bank on the morning of those days at latest. Now, however, steamers sail almost daily. The mails to South America are fairly frequent, sometimes two or three in a week, while the overland route to Japan, *viâ* Siberia, has naturally greatly facilitated the means of communication between this country and the Far East.

A very important section that falls to be dealt with under this heading is the subject of credits ; but beyond a brief reference to there is no necessity here for any lengt exposition. It is sufficient to say that for t purpose of facilitating the negotiation of b drawn against produce by exporters abro credits are frequently arranged by the impo here with the leading banks or discount merchant houses. This enables the exp abroad to at once have perfect security business, and to obtain the best paper. A commission for charged by the bank issuing t drafts drawn, at rates which tween the bank and the impor against the bills drawn are, as a rule, made by telegraphic transfer, this being the cheaper course for all parties concerned, rather than by the slow process of mail remittances.

It may not be out of place to refer here to the proposed International Conference on the unification of the laws relating to bills of exchange in different countries. The rule which deals with what is perhaps the most popularly known and understood amongst the various rules suggested is that which proposes hat no days of grace shall be allowed. Should his become law there will be a disappearance our old friend the conundrum, " On what te does a two months' bill, dated 31st ?cember, mature ? "

SECTION II.

LOANS, OVERDRAFTS, Etc.

A vast subject is included under this simple heading, but, as the reader has already been informed, this work does not profess to be of a technical nature, and is intended rather as a guide-book or work of ready reference. It is, therefore, not proposed to enter into the various intricacies that surround the subject, but rather to state, briefly and concisely, the various kinds of loans, or, more correctly, the various classes of securities against which loans are made, how such loans are to be applied for, and the points to be borne in mind when the applications are made.

As regards unsecured overdrafts or loans, it is unnecessary to do more than merely mention them. They are comparatively rare, and are allowed only to those whose standing is undoubted.

(1.) *Bills of Exchange.*—This stands in the forefront of advances made by banks, but as bills are dealt with in a separate section it is unnecessary to make any reference to the subject here beyond mere passing comment. Just as there are higher and lower grades of Stock Exchange securities, so also there are varying degrees of quality in bills of exchange, from bank bills and fine trade bills down through the "rank and file" of ordinary commercial paper to the humblest class of bill; whilst below all these there are the bills which it is desirable and necessary to avoid. Advances are made against bills in various ways (by purchase, loan, etc.); and the charges for such advances naturally vary according to the class and currency of the paper, the status of the borrower, and the market rates for the time being as they appear in the daily papers.

(2.) *Loans against Stock Exchange Securities.* —Next to advances against bills this may perhaps be regarded, from a banker's point of view, as a most favoured class of loan, for the simple reason that such securities can be so readily realised. Of course we are now speaking of the better class of securities. As a rule banks will not make loans against mining

shares or against securities the prices of which
are not quoted on the Stock Exchange Official
List; and if they depart from this rule it is
only under exceptional circumstances and in
cases where the loan is granted more upon the
ground of the respectability of the customer
than upon the nature of the security he offers.
In fact the question of the character of the
customer enters more or less into any kind of
loan that may be made to him. While, however, a banker may have, in some rare cases,
to refuse an advance of this kind, he has
nevertheless a very large number of customer
who, from various causes, require loans for ‹
shorter or longer period against their Stoc]
Exchange securities; and in a general wa\
and within proper limits, these can be readi
obtained. You call on your banker, say,´
ask for an advance of £300 in respect of s‹
foreign bonds you hold. He will requir
know for how long you will want the ‘
and if for a‚longer period than is custon
he will probably fix a time, say three or
months, telling you that if at the end of
period you require a renewal for the who
part of the amount advanced you should·
a fresh application. Keep a note of the

D

before you, and either see your bank manager or write to him a few days beforehand, stating what are your wishes in the matter. Some customers are careless on this point, and allow the date to pass by without taking the least notice; when written to they will reply that the matter had escaped them and they would like the loan, or part of it, to be continued for so much longer. Others again intend to pay off the loan when due, but are under the impression that the banker will recoup himself by debiting their current account. They ·hould, however, remember that such a course vould be irregular, and that the proper method ·s for them to draw a cheque on their current ·ccount for the amount of the loan (that is, of ourse, assuming that there is sufficient in the ·ount) and to forward it to the manager, who ᵗ in due course charge their account with amount of interest due.

·r those who are in doubt upon the point— there are such—it may be well to mention · that a borrower can, of course, pay off whole, or part, of his loan if he should ·e to do so, *before* the date fixed for its ·ment. Interest is of course only charge-·co the date of repayment.

Suppose, again, that the advance you require is against railway stock or other registered stock or shares standing in your name, your banker will require you to execute a transfer in favour of the bank or of its nominees, such transfer and the relative certificate of course being deposited in his hands. If the loan be a small one, or only temporary, the banker will possibly keep them in that form; but if the loan be for a large amount or for more than a temporary period, he will probably lodge the transfer for registration; and the stock or shares will of course be re-transferred to yor when the loan is paid off. The consideratio money on the transfer being nominal, th stamp duty will be 10s. and the compan\ registration fee is usually 2s. 6d., so that y will have 12s. 6d. to pay both when the lc is made to you and again when it is rep‹ Should the securities be registered in name or names of some one other than yor —say, for example, in the name of your who is willing for the bank to make an adv —the bank would require a special letter the wife authorising them to make an adv; such letter to be signed at the same time th executes the transfer of the stock or sha:

When arranging the loan with your banker, whether against bonds or registered securities, you will find that he will require a "margin" of say from 15 to 20 per cent. ; that is to say, supposing he were making you a loan of £300 against Chinese 6 per cent. gold bonds he would require bonds to the value of about £350 to be lodged. This gives a "margin" of about 15 per cent., and allows for any depreciation that may take place in the price. With a security liable to greater fluctuations, or of an inferior description, he might possibly require a somewhat larger margin. The question of the rate of interest is also a point that will be arranged at the time of your applying for the loan. Such charges are generally on a sliding scale, and vary with the rise or fall of the bank rate; that is to the charge to you would be most probably at so much per cent. above bank rate, a minimum of so much per cent. per im. You will also require to sign what called a "memorandum of deposit," or rrowed note" (to be stamped, 6d.), a comtively simple document, setting forth that ich a day you have borrowed, say from 'ornhill and Leadenhall Bank, the sum of so much against securities as specified, at such a rate and repayable by such a date, and that upon failure to repay the loan by the specified date, or that if, during the currency of the loan, the required margin is not maintained, the bank is authorised to sell the securities, or any others which may be substituted for them ; any deficiency after such realisation also to be made good to the bank. As a matter of fact, the bank would not, under ordinary circumstances, sell the securities without first notifying the borrower that their value was below the required margin. Where such notifications have to be made from time to time the borrower either repays a portion of the loan, or sends in additional cover to the bank. But if the borrower takes no action and the securities continue to fall, the bank, to protect itself against loss, may find it necessary to sell the securities before they have shrunk to a price that is less than the amount loaned against them.

The whole process of loans against Stock Exchange securities, from start to finish, is thus, in practice, a very simple matter. The arrangement with the manager for the loan and the preparation and signature of the various forms is, over and over again, merely a matter of a few minutes ; and when the loan is repaid the borrower can, if he chooses, for his own satisfaction ask his banker whether the forms that he signed at the time when the advance was made have been cancelled and filed. Whether he makes the enquiries or not, he may rest satisfied that this has been done.

(3) *Loans against Deeds.*—Whilst bankers are always prepared to make advances to a certain extent against deeds relating to land, house property, etc., it will be readily understood that this class of business is less in favour with them than certain other kinds of loan because the security offered cannot be so readily realised. It may be said that both the loans and the deeds securing them are of a less liquid nature than those of any kind we have previously discussed, and naturally a larger margin will be required than on Stock Exchange securities. Moreover, advances against deeds are generally required for a longer period that those made against Stock Exchange securities. In several simple cases there is no necessity for the deeds to be examined by the bank's solicitors ; but where there are several

documents or the title is at all involved the bank will, as a matter of course, require its solicitors to examine and report thereon; and consequently some time may elapse before everything is clear and the loan can be made. As in the case of loans against Stock Exchange securities, your banker will require you to execute a memorandum of deposit, the stamp duty thereon being 1s. per cent., or in some cases 2s. 6d. per cent., on the amount advanced. When applying for an advance against deeds of property that is insured, remember that the bank will also require a fire policy to be lodged with the deeds, together with the receipt showing the last premium thereon to have been paid. They will attend to the payment of future premiums for you if you request them to do so; but it is preferable that the customer should attend to it. Again, if the advance required is against deeds relating to leasehold property, you must also produce, when making your application, the receipt for last payment of ground rent; and during the continuance of the loan you will require to forward to the bank the succeeding receipts for ground rents. Sometimes these receipts can only be borrowed; where such is the case the bank will probably be satisfied with their production and will return them after they have been exhibited. This remark also applies in the case of premium receipts where the insurance is attended to by the ground landlord.

It is scarcely necessary to add that where the property concerned comes within the area of the Land Registry Office and the scope of the Acts under which it has been established, the bank will also require the land certificate to be deposited with them. In the ordinary course they will advise the Registry Office of such deposit, withdrawing the notice when their advance has been repaid. For a simple notice of deposit the Land Registry charge 1s.

(4) *Loans against Dock Warrants and Bills of Lading.*—This is a still " less general " class of business, and the percentage of advances that come under this heading is comparatively small. A few very general remarks will therefore suffice. One of the main points tó remember is that your banker will be sure to ask you for the policy covering the goods when you take your warrants or bills of lading to apply for the advance. If, therefore, you have the policy

by you, you should take it with you. If the goods are covered inclusively with others, and you are unable to lodge the policy, or the bank already holds it in connection with a previous advance, you should be prepared to give the particulars of the policy. Warrants and bills of lading both require endorsement. The duration of a loan will to some extent depend upon the nature of the goods; where, for example, they are easily perishable, or in cases where they are of such a nature that they ought not to remain long in bond or warehouse, a banker will naturally enquire of his customer if the warrants are not taken out of his hands within a reasonable time. In regard to this class of advances, also, special memorandum forms of deposit have to be signed.

Sometimes, instead of the warrants or bills of lading being held by the banker, they are deposited with the wharfinger or dock company, to whom instructions are given to hold the goods at the sole disposal of the bank. When goods thus held are to be released, wholly or in part, the borrower obtains his banker's signature to a delivery order addressed to the dock company or wharfinger.

(5.) *Loans against Guarantees.*—Sometimes
a bank makes a loan to a person, firm or company against the guarantee of some reliable
person or against the joint and several
guarantee of persons of undoubted standing.
In such cases close inquiries are of course
made of the bankers of the guarantors. When
the loan is paid off the guarantee is cancelled
and filed. Under the Statute of Limitations
it used to be necessary to renew guarantees
at the expiration of six years; this, however,
is generally now averted by the special form of
guarantee. Of course there are cases when
collateral security is required to the guarantee.
In the event of the death of a guarantor,
whether the guarantee has been given by him
solely, or jointly with others, the loan usually
becomes repayable, but arrangements can, of
course, be made for a new guarantee to be
given by the executors of the deceased
guarantor, or by the survivors in the joint
account, where all parties to the transaction
are agreeable.

(6.) *Loans against Life Policies.*—This again
is a somewhat limited class of advance. It is
a rule with banks in these cases to send a

notice to the insurance office advising them of the fact that the policy has been assigned to the bank against an advance, and requesting that such notice shall be entered on the company's books. The company forward, in due course, to the bank, their acknowledgment of such notice. When the loan is repaid the policy is re-assigned to the customer, such re-assignment being usually endorsed on the form which the customer signed when lodging the policy with the bank.

It should be noted by the customer that if the age has not already been admitted on the policy on which he requires an advance, he should obtain and furnish the bank with a certificate of birth.

(7.) *Advances for Payment of Estate Duty.*— Sometimes an advance is required by the executor of a deceased person to enable him to pay Estate Duty. In such cases it is customary to sign a simple form of agreement stating that in consideration of the sum advanced the borrower charges all the property, in respect of which the duty is payable, with the repayment to the bank on demand of the sum thus lent, with interest, and undertakes to execute, if required by the bank, a mortgage of the said property to the bank. This last contingency is scarcely likely to arise, as, in a general way, the amount is not borrowed until it has actually to be paid over to the Inland Revenue, and immediately the Probate Grant has been obtained, the executor can of course at once deal with the property, and pay off the loan from the bank.

We have dealt under the foregoing seven headings with the principal classes of securities against which advances are made; but there are, of course, various other kinds of security upon which bankers grant loans, such as documentary bills, bills lodged for collection, promissory notes, ships, reversions, etc., etc.; while there are doubtless several others of a still more exceptional nature, and in some instances peculiar to the locality in which loans from the local banks are obtained thereon. It may perhaps also be well to add here that there are certain "securities" against which a bank should *not* be expected to advance; such, for instance, as jewellery or household furniture.

In concluding the remarks contained in this chapter on loans, a quotation from an article which appeared in the *Banker's Magazine* may not be out of place :—

" Almost the commonest misconception of the rank and file of a bank's customers with regard to the functions of a bank, is that of confounding a bank loan with a permanent mortgage. They cannot understand why, when the bank has good security, it should want reductions of the loans it makes ; and certainly, if the local manager does enter into the views of the head office, he often does not relish having to enforce them. Another requirement, which is often found hard to carry out, is the stipulation that an adequate balance should be maintained on the current account of the borrower. The latter does not see why, if he pays interest on his loan, he should keep a portion lying unproductive on current account, quite overlooking the bank's claim to remuneration in respect of that account. To impress upon the customer the justice of these views and claims of the bank is the duty of its manager.''

CHAPTER III.

———

BANK OF ENGLAND.

CHAPTER III.

THE BANK OF ENGLAND.

So many thousands of persons scattered throughout the country are holders of Government, Colonial or other stocks inscribed at the Bank of England, that a special chapter containing some of the principal rules and regulations relating to such stocks will undoubtedly prove of considerable service to the many who are interested therein. Within the compass of this small work it is impossible to comprise all that could be written under this heading, or to give specimens of the many forms required for various purposes. It will, however, be found that all the salient points which concern the stockholder are dealt with in this chapter. Ampler particulars, if required, will be found in " The Country Banker's Handbook."

No useful purpose would perhaps be served in giving here a list of all the stocks, the books of which are kept at the Bank of England ; and

E

it is assumed that if the reader holds any such stock or stocks, he is aware of their being so inscribed and of the dates when the dividends thereon become due. We will, therefore, proceed to discuss first, the mode of *"Transfer of Stocks."*

Certain Indian Railway Debenture Stocks, together with other stocks, are transferable by deed. For Consols, Indian, Colonial, Corporation, and in fact for the majority of stocks, the usual form is by transfer on the bank books. The *modus operandi* is somewhat as follows:— The stockbroker who receives the order, say to sell a £1,000-Consols, lodges what is called a "ticket" with the bank, giving particulars of the names, etc., of buyer and seller. The bank then prepare a transfer form on their Consols Register, and between 12 and 3 o'clock (Saturdays excepted) the seller or his attorney calls at the bank and signs the transfer book and a stock receipt which gives particulars of the transfer, and then hands such receipt to the stockbroker, who in turn passes it on, against payment, to the broker for the purchaser.

We have used the expression above "the seller, or his attorney." If the seller is non-resident in London, and he has, for example, given instructions to his banker to sell the stock for him, he will require them at the same time to obtain a power of attorney which will enable one of the principal officers of the bank's head office in London to attend at the Bank of England, and there to sign the transfer book on the seller's behalf. (As to the form in which you should give your bank instructions, either to sell or to purchase stocks inscribed at the Bank of England, see "Investments" section, pp. 67-69.) In this connection it may be well to mention that applications for power of attorney have to be lodged by hand at the Bank of England, and must not be sent through the post. Another point worth bearing in mind is, that where you desire to sell or transfer only a *portion* of the stock you hold you can, if you so wish, obtain a power to cover the *whole* amount, and then sell or transfer portions at a time. Remembrance of this fact may save the cost of several unnecessary powers where one would be sufficient, but at the same time, it must also be borne in mind that a power will become obsolete if five years are allowed to elapse between the dates when it is acted upon.

Further notes under this heading may be summarised as follows :—

(1) A sale power covers both sale and *transfer*, therefore any part of the stock named in the power can be sold and the balance transferred into some other name or names if so desired.

(2) The bank will not accept *general* powers of attorney in place of their own special form.

(3) When giving instructions for sale or transfer powers, it must be remembered that where the stock stands in the name of a deceased holder, his address and description as on the bank books must be stated, as well as the names of his executors or administrator.

(4) Where there are two or more names in the account, the *order* in which such names stand must appear on the application form.

Dividend Payments.—In the absence of any instructions to the contrary, the Bank of England send warrants by post to the sole or first-named stockholder (sole stockholder includes sole surviving stockholder, sole executor or administrator, and sole surviving executor or administrator; first stockholder includes first executor).

Should you desire, however, your dividends to be otherwise forwarded, or to be received by your bankers, you will find that the latter has in all probability a supply of the necessary forms of request that require to be signed in order that dividends may be so forwarded. If it is your wish that your banker should collect your dividends for you, the request form, when signed, should be sent or handed to him, in order that he may enter particulars on his register and transmit it to his head office for lodgment with the Bank of England. This will save you all further trouble in the matter, and you will find that dividends will be regularly placed to your account. Moreover, such dividend request will remain in force, and no fresh form will be required, although the stock may be added to, or a portion of it sold. Also, should there be any back dividends to be collected, your banker can obtain them under these forms.

A dividend request becomes void—

(1) By sale or transfer of the stock.
(2) By the death of a sole stockholder or of the last survivor in the account.

(3) By the division of an account into two or more designated accounts.

There are also other circumstances under which the authority may become void, but the above are the principal.

Facilities are given for investment through the Bank of England of dividends on Consols, Local Loans, Indian and certain other stocks, full particulars of which, together with forms and instructions, you can readily obtain through your banker. Arrangements can also be made for the investment of dividends on stocks standing in the names of minors, and in this case also forms and particulars can be procured in the same way.

As regards unclaimed dividends and stocks, should you be an enquirer for such, it will be well that you should ask your banker to supply you with copies of the Bank of England's circulars and forms of application for the recovery of such dividends.

Death, how to prove.—The bank's requirements are too lengthy to give here in detail. There are special regulations which have to be observed in the case of a stockholder, or an executor or an administrator of a stockholder, who dies or is buried abroad. The salient points, however, may be summarised as follows :—

(1) Either probate of will or letters of administration must be exhibited at the bank in the case of a shareholder in a sole account, or of the last survivor in a joint account.

(2) Where probates or letters of administration have already been exhibited to the bank, but the death is subsequently required to be proved on some other stock inscribed there, the quotation of the Bank of England's mark on the probate will generally suffice.

(3) When lodging probate, full particulars of the amount and description of stock and the name or names in which it stands must be supplied.

(4) In the case of joint accounts, or where there is a surviving stockholder, or a surviving executor or administrator of a stockholder, left in the account, (*a*) probate or letters of administration, (*b*) a certified burial extract, or (*c*) a death certificate issued by the General Registrar of London, Dublin or Edinburgh must be lodged, and the bank,

where necessary, will prepare statutory declarations of identity, or of comparison and identity, as the case may be.

(5) Where death or burial takes place beyond the limits of the United Kingdom, the probate or letters of administration must be granted or sealed by His Majesty's High Court of Justice, Principal Registry, and all Colonial grants must be sealed by the English Court.

(6) Where the deceased died in a foreign country and there is in the account a surviving stockholder, or an administrator or an executor of a stockholder, death must be proved (*a*) by probate or letters of administration, or by reference to any bank marks thereon, or to an account in which deceased's death has been already registered, (*b*) by an extract of the registry of burials kept by the British Chaplain, or (*c*) by a certificate of death or burial in accordance with the law of the country in which deceased died.

If the deceased died in British India, or in a British Colony or Dependency, (*a*) by exhibition of probate or letters of administration as mentioned in clause (*a*)

above, (*b*) a certificate of death or burial
in accordance with the law of the place
in which deceased died, (*c*) reference to
an account in which his death has
already been registered.

Where necessary declarations of identity
will be prepared by the registry office of the
Bank of England.

Bear in mind that the name of a stockholder
is not removed from the bank books by his
death being proved.

Sometimes stock in respect of which death
has to be proved is a trustee account, and
exceeds, either in itself, or when added to other
stocks, the amount of personal estate mentioned
in the probate on which duty has been paid.
In such cases the Bank of England require a
separate affidavit to be made in accordance
with a form which they supply.

When probate or letters of administration
are lodged with the bank they require forms
to be signed by the executors or administrators; and it is well to note that in the event
of your banker proving death for you at the
Bank of England, those forms he will send
you for signature—assuming that you are an
executor—must be returned direct to him

and not to the Bank of England. In fact, it will save considerable trouble, in the event of a solicitor proving death for you at the Bank of England, or at any other place where proof of death has to be lodged, if he (the solicitor) will entrust the business to his own banker. The latter will send probate, or death certificate, or whatever it may be, together with stock certificates, dividend warrants, or other documents that have to be produced, to his head office, who will do whatever is necessary in the matter.

A few other points that may be noted under this heading are : (1) Death in a sole account, or of the last survivor in a joint account, renders the then existing dividend request forms void. (2) In a joint account in which there is at least one surviving stockholder the deceased stockholder's name can be removed if so desired (*i.e.*, when death has been proved in the bank books) upon the execution of a special form by the surviving stockholder or stockholders. These forms can be readily obtained from your banker, and the removal of a name gives the advantage, should it be required, of making a further addition to the stock which would otherwise be impracticable,

as a "deceased" account cannot be added to.
(3) If a stockholder, at the time of his death,
had a dividend warrant in his possession, such
warrant should be lodged with the proof of
death, and a new one will be issued in its
place. The executors or administrators will
not, however, receive it, in the ordinary course,
until about six weeks after the warrant has
been lodged with the bank; but the amount
can be received, almost immediately, by your
banker's head office upon lodgment of a dividend request form, or it can be obtained early
if the executor will write especially for it.
(4) In cases of cremation the bank will accept a
certified extract from the Records of Cremation,
which must be supported by a declaration of
comparison and identity prepared by the bank.

Miscellaneous.—Indian Government Rupee
Loans practically constitute a department by
themselves in the Bank of England. These
Rupee securities are held in one of three forms;
they are (*a*) Promissory Notes, or are (*b*)
inscribed on the Bank of England books, or
they are (*c*) Stock Certificates to bearer
with coupons attached. The dividends on
promissory notes and inscribed stock are paid

by Bills of Exchange on India, commonly called Interest Bills ; and as such bills and coupons are payable in India in rupees, they are generally sold in London, for sterling, at the exchange of the day, through a banker or other agent. Should you be a holder of Rupee stock, and require income tax certificates in respect of your interest payments, you can obtain them on applying to your banker, just the same as in the case of British sterling stocks.

Where it is desired to open a corporate account in any stock inscribed at the bank, a special form, which your banker can supply, will have to be executed.

Special request forms have also to be executed under the following circumstances :—

By a shareholder who is described as "spinster" or "widow," for the alteration of her name and description on marriage.

For permission to hold stock in the same name(s) in two, three, or four accounts.

To open a separate account for stock about to be transferred.

For the alteration of the address of a stockholder, or of a nominee, to whom dividend warrants are sent.

For the amalgamation of two or more accounts.

For the verification of stock accounts at the Bank of England.

For the removal of the name of a stockholder, whose death has been proved, from a joint account in which there is at least one survivor.

A few words respecting some of the special forms may be serviceable. As regards the request for alteration of name, etc., on marriage, it should be noted that the bank does not require the production of a marriage certificate; also, that if the stockholder desires that the existing dividend request in favour of her banker should still remain in force, she should state it on the form (mentioning the name of such bank) immediately above the place for signature.

As regards the change of address forms, it is considered best, in a general way, not to alter the *original* address; although for *postal* purposes it may be necessary to alter the address on the bank books. Stockholders are of course at liberty to do as they please in the matter; but through removal they frequently give trouble to themselves and others by their

non-recollection of the address in which their
stock actually stands.

With regard to the amalgamation of accounts, if the dividend request forms on such
accounts be in favour of different persons it
should be stated on the amalgamation form
which of the dividend requests is to be in force
on the joint account.

With reference to the request to hold stock
in the same name(s) in two or more accounts, it
should be noted that a designated account cannot
be " split " except by transfer in the usual way,
nor can designated accounts be amalgamated.

As regards the request for verification of
accounts, the bank's charge for this service is
6d. an account, with a minimum fee of 1s. per
certificate.   The request should always be
signed by one of the stockholders, whether it
is required that the reply should be addressed
to himself, to a co-stockholder, or to some other
person or firm.   Where the stock stands in
the name of a corporation, the chairman,
secretary, or other officer should sign.   This
regulation may be taken generally as holding
good, not only as regards stocks inscribed at
the Bank of England, but also in respect of
stocks inscribed or registered at other banks.

CHAPTER IV.

INVESTMENTS, Etc.

CHAPTER IV.—SECTION I.

STOCK EXCHANGE TRANSACTIONS THROUGH BANKERS.

FOR the large number of bank customers who hold Stock Exchange securities it may be of assistance if a few simple rules are given as to the form which their instructions for the sale or purchase of securities should take. Before, however, proceeding to the consideration of these, it is desirable to mention one very important fact which cannot be too widely known, namely, that in Stock Exchange business for a customer, it is the banker, and not the customer, who takes the risk of the broker being unable to meet his engagements. In view of this, and of the fact that it is the banker who handles and transmits the orders, makes or receives payments, and forwards the bonds, certificates, transfers, etc., the banker is very fairly entitled to the half commission charged, which he receives

F

from the broker. This arrangement is a great convenience to the customer, for he only pays exactly the same commission as if he had gone direct to the broker, and he is saved both trouble and risk. To the broker, also, the arrangement is a satisfactory one ; for while he pays half of his commission to the banker he receives a large number of orders which would never have come into his hands otherwise, and he also is saved trouble and risk. Thus is explained the expression, "Brokerage divisible with the Bank," which appears on contract notes for purchase and sale of securities by a customer through his banker ; as also, why the contract notes are made out in the bank's name, and not that of the customer.

We will now assume that you have money you wish to invest, and, having decided upon the securities you intend to purchase—possibly with the guidance or assistance of your banker—you write to, or call upon, him with the request that he will effect the purchase through his brokers accordingly. In this case it will help you if you know :—

(1) That your instructions should always be in writing, and should contain an

authority that your account, or such account as you may name, is to be debited with the cost of purchase.

(2) If you intend to buy bearer bonds, the amount in sterling of such bonds should be given. For instance, to ask your banker to buy "two Japanese 4 per cent. bonds" would leave him in doubt as to whether you meant two £50, £100, or £1,000 bonds, or whatever denomination the bonds required might happen to be.

(3) If the order is for the purchase of registered stocks or shares, always quote in full the name, address and occupation in which such stocks or shares are to be registered. As regards "occupation" this should be stated, where a lady is the buyer, as "spinster," "married woman," or "widow."

(4) If the stock to be purchased is inscribed at the Bank of England, always state, in your instructions for its purchase, whether you already hold any of the same stock, as the banker, in passing on the order to his broker, is always

required to state whether it is for an
" old account " or " new account."

On the other hand, supposing you have
securities to sell, you will request your banker
to instruct his brokers to dispose of such
securities and to credit your account, or such
account as you mention, when he receives the
proceeds. You will then :—

(1) If you are selling bearer bonds, hand or
forward such bonds to him, or take a
note to do so three or four days before
the settling day; or, should the bonds
already be held by the banker on your
behalf, you will remind him that they
are in his possession.

(2) If your order is for the sale of registered
stocks or shares, you will deal similarly
with the certificate as with the bonds
above mentioned, taking care to point
out to the banker if your present
address differs from that given on the
certificate.

(3) Should the stock which you desire to
dispose of be inscribed on the books of
the Bank of England, the Crown
Agents for the Colonies, the London
and Westminster Bank, Limited, the

National Provincial Bank of England, Limited, or any other office where, in the absence of personal attendance, a power of attorney for sale is required, you must give the full names, addresses, and occupations as on the register of the stock, asking your banker to obtain the necessary power, and to sell the stock either " for return of the power," or after he has received the power back duly executed. Of course, if you are resident in London, you will probably prefer to attend at the bank at which the stock is inscribed, and to sign the book there accordingly. For this purpose you have simply to fix the day and hour (usually between 1 and 3 p.m., Saturdays excepted) with your banker.

It will be found that the above simple rules practically cover the ground of the requisite form of order for purchase or sale of stocks and shares. There are, however, some variations from these, such as, for instance, when a purchaser wishes to invest an exact amount of money. This, of course, cannot be done as regards shillings and pence, or, perhaps, even a few pounds, where bearer bonds are purchased ; but several Government, Colonial and Corporation stocks can be purchased to absorb exact sums to a penny. Similarly also it is sometimes desired to sell so much stock as, including all expenses, will realise an exact amount, and to this also the above remarks with regard to the investment of an exact sum apply. Any little difficulty that you may find in these matters, your bankers will always readily help you with.

There are certain points that it is well to observe when giving orders for the sale or purchase of stock, and it is necessary that these should always be so worded as to avoid any possibility of misunderstanding. Sometimes, for instance, a banker is asked to buy one Great Northern Railway share, or £100 worth of India $3\frac{1}{2}$ per cent. stock, leaving him in doubt as to what is in the mind of his customer; whether he means £100 stock as regards the Great Northern Railway, and if his intention is that £100 India $3\frac{1}{2}$ per cent. stock should be purchased, or £100 money invested in the stock.

Whenever you are buying or selling registered stocks or shares, it will be well to bear in mind that ten days are allowed after settling day, in accordance with the rules of the Stock Exchange, for the delivery of such transfer. That is to say, if you are a purchaser, ten days may elapse before you get your transfer deed for execution; or if you are a seller—and possibly the shares held may be registered in two or three other names jointly with your own—you will have ten days in which to sign and return the transfer. When you have returned the transfer deed for the stocks or shares purchased, you should allow some three weeks or a month for the preparation of the certificate.

Perhaps it might prove of some interest to the reader if a definition were given here of the meaning of the terms "inscribed" and "registered," which have been so frequently used. Without going too exactly into details, the word "inscribed" is usually applied to stocks which, like Consols, are transferable on books, either in person or by power of attorney; while the term "registered" is applied to stocks and shares that are transferable by the ordinary transfer deed.

It may also be of advantage to point out that, while Consols and various British Government and Colonial stocks are usually sold for cash, it is customary to sell bearer bonds and registered stocks and shares for the settlement. Small amounts of stock are sometimes sold for cash, and in such cases it frequently happens that the word "free" is added after the price on the contract note, which means that the jobber takes the stock into his own name free of stamp duty and fee to himself; these have therefore to be paid by the seller, and accordingly are deducted from the proceeds.

Where you are the holder of Colonial inscribed stocks it is always well, in the event of sale, to quote the year, as well as the rate per cent., of the stock which you hold. Reference to your stock receipt should enable you to give this information.

Should you give an order to your bankers for sale and purchase of different stocks at the same time, you will be charged commission only on one side of the transaction. This would also be the case should there be the lapse of a few days between sale and purchase, provided both transactions take place during the same account; but in this event you should give your banker, when forwarding the second

order, a reminder of the previous recent sale
or purchase on your behalf.

A remark may be made with advantage on
the subject of "limits" which are frequently
imposed when instructions are given for the
sale or purchase of stocks. While, of course,
a customer has a perfect right, if he chooses, to
impose such limits, he sometimes defeats his
own ends by quoting an impracticable price.
Thus, where he desires to sell, the quotation
may continue to drop, or if he desires to
purchase, the price may gradually rise ; whereas just a fraction lower or higher, as the case
might be, would have secured the desired
object. Sometimes a little guidance from
your bankers may help you in this direction.
In this connection you will also do well to
bear in mind that stock orders with limits do
not necessarily expire at the settlement, but
remain in force until they are executed or
until instructions are given by you that they
should be cancelled.

If you are purchasing or selling foreign
bonds with coupons payable abroad, rupee
stocks or American railway shares, you will
do well to bear in mind that Dutch bonds are
reckoned at the rate of 12 guilders to the

pound, French and Italian at 25 francs and 25 lire respectively, German at 20 marks, United States at $5 to the pound, Japanese at 2s. 0½d. per yen, and the rupee at 2s. for stock and 1s. 4d. for interest. As regards the last named, when rupee stocks are bought it is customary for the accrued interest up to the date of settlement to be added to the cost, or, in the case of a sale, to be added to the proceeds.

Should you be a holder of American railroad shares, it may be well to point out to you that it is considered advisable, for some reasons, to have such shares registered in the holders' own names. By this means considerable trouble and difficulty is saved in the collection of dividends from the persons or firms whose names would otherwise appear on the certificates; and the risk of transmission of such certificates every time a dividend has to be claimed, with the possible event of a small commission being charged for paying the dividend, is thus avoided. Should you decide to have the shares registered in your own name, your bankers will undertake the matter for you, and you should instruct them whether they are to be insured, as well as registered, in transit to and from America. You can also arrange with your bankers for the receipt of dividends by them, in the event of your not wishing the dividends to be forwarded to you direct. A further advisable step to take when you receive the share certificates, registered in your own name, is to at once endorse them with your name exactly as stated on the face of the certificate, " without alteration or enlargement or any change whatever," taking care also that the witness to your signature adds his full address and description immediately beneath his own signature. If you leave the certificates unendorsed, at the time of your death heavy expense and considerable delay in sending proof of your death out to America would be incurred before the shares could be dealt with. The shares would of necessity require to be endorsed if at any time you were to ask your banker to make an advance upon them, or to sell them.

But, while on the subject of American railway shares, it is only right to point out that at present an anomaly exists as regards the two classes of "market name" and "own name" shares. It may be briefly explained thus:—While for the purposes of delivery

American railway shares are "bearer" documents, they are "registered" so far as dividends and "rights" are concerned. For these last-named purposes it is, therefore, advantageous to the buyer to have the shares registered in his "own name"; on the other hand, if he wishes to sell the shares it may prove a disadvantage to him, seeing that the buyer will probably prefer certificates bearing a "market name" (*i.e.*, of some large London firm), for the reason that he can readily claim dividends and "rights" from the latter, whereas he may have difficulty in finding the whereabouts of the seller, whose address does not appear on the certificate. The anomaly would very largely disappear if *all* purchasers were to have the shares registered in their own names, and gave instructions to the railway companies for payment of dividends to their bankers.

Probably the reader is already aware that the Stock Exchange settlement occurs twice a month, that is about the middle and end of each month; the actual dates you will be able readily to ascertain from the columns of one or other of the money articles of the daily papers. The settlement is spread over four

days, the first two being occupied with arranging rates, while on the third or "ticket day"
the broker must be supplied with the names,
etc., for registered stocks and shares purchased
during the past account, if they have not already
been given to him. The fourth day is what
may be termed "settling day" proper, and
accounts are then settled between bankers and
brokers for securities purchased and sold on
account of branches or customers, while the
securities purchased, and transfers in respect
of stocks or shares sold, are handed by the
brokers to the bankers. Sometimes a delay of
one or two days may happen as regards the
delivery of transfers which are prepared by the
companies themselves, but these are somewhat
exceptional cases. The seller is allowed ten
days, dating from the settling day, for the
execution of the transfers of shares or stocks
which he has sold ; but if not completed and in
the hands of the brokers by that time, the stock
is then liable to be "bought in." Here it may
be convenient to remind some that where they
have sold and bought during the same account
they should not retain the sale transfers until
transfers for the purchases reach them. As
regards transactions for "special settlement,"

which usually have reference to the scrip of a new loan, or the shares or stock of some new company, the appointment of such special settling days is announced from week to week, and generally appears in the Tuesday morning money market column of the leading London dailies, and in the financial papers.

Two Stock Exchange regulations with reference to "bad delivery" may here be quoted. One has reference to writing the customer's name on the back or face of bearer bonds. This must not be done under any circumstances, nor should even an india-rubber stamp with the purchaser's name be impressed on a bond or coupons. The other is to the effect that, should a broker deliver a drawn bond to a purchaser he is liable to make good any loss which may ensue in the purchase of a fresh bond to replace the one drawn.

In addition to the ordinary bank holidays, there are also three "fixed" Stock Exchange holidays in the course of the year, namely, 1st January, 1st May, and 1st November, or on the day following should either of those dates occur on a Sunday. There are also occasional dates on which the Stock Exchange is closed, of which notice is always given a few days beforehand in the money article of the daily papers, and in the financial papers.

A word or two may be said here as regards the "Forged Transfers Acts, 1891-92," in connection with British railways. A large number of these have adopted the Acts, but make no charge. The following companies, however, namely, the London & Blackwall, the London Chatham & Dover, and the Rhymney, charge 1d. for every £25 or fractional part of £25 of all stocks conveyed, except that the London Chatham & Dover Railway charges 1d. for every £100 of Ordinary Stock and 1d. for every £50 of Second Preference Stock.*

The following tables giving the usual scale of brokerage, and also a note of certain stamp duties, will probably prove of service :—

SCALE OF BROKERAGE.

British and Foreign Funds... ...	$\frac{1}{8}$% on Stock.
Bank of England Stock	$\{ \begin{array}{l} \frac{1}{8}\% \text{ on Money or} \\ \frac{1}{4}\% \text{ on Stock.} \end{array}$
Corporation Stocks and Bonds ...	
Colonial „ „ ...	
Rupee Paper	$\frac{1}{4}$% on Stock.
Foreign Railway Bonds	
American Bonds	

---

* The London Chatham & Dover do not now make any charge.

Railway and other Stocks :—

Over £50 per cent.	... ...	½% on Money.
From £50 to £25 per cent.	...	¼% on Stock.
Under £25 ...	... ...	⅛% on Stock.

American Railway Shares :—   s.   d. per share.

					s.	d.
Under the value of $5		...	...		0	1½
Of the value of $5 and under $10			...		0	3
„	10	„	25	...	0	6
„	25	„	50	...	0	9
„	50	„	75	...	1	0
„	75	„	100	...	1	3
„	100	„	125	...	1	6
„	125	„	150	...	2	0
„	150	„	200	...	2	6
$200 and over		...	...	...	½% on Money.	

Minimum Commission charge, 2s. 6d.

All other Shares :—

		£	s.		£	s.	per share.
Under the value of		0	10			...	1½d.
Of the value of		0	10	and under	1	5 ...	3d.
„	„	1	5	„	2	10 ...	6d.
„	„	2	10	„	5	0 ...	9d.
„	„	5	0	„	7	10 ...	1/-
„	„	7	10	„	10	0 ...	1/3
„	„	10	0	„	15	0 ...	1/6
„	„	15	0	„	20	0 ...	2/-
„	„	20	0	„	25	0 ...	2/6
Above £25 ...		...	...	...	...	½% on Money.	

(For transferring, as distinct from selling, Stocks or
Shares :—Half the above rates.)

*STAMPS ON CONTRACT NOTES.

Where consideration money is under £5 ... Nil.

,, ,, ,, is £5 and under £100 ...1d.

,, ,, ,, is £100 $^{up\ to}_{any}$ amount ...1/-

Where a Note advises the sale or purchase of more than one description of Stock or marketable security, the Note shall be deemed to be as many Contract Notes as there are descriptions of stock or security sold or purchased.

STAMP DUTIES.

Conveyance or transfer on sale :

Not exceeding	£5	...	...	...	...	6d.
,,	10	...	...	...	...	-/
,,	15	...	...	...	..	1/6
,,	20	...	...	...	...	2/-
,,	25	...	...	...	...	2/6
,,	50	...	...	...	...	5/-

for every additional £25 up to £300 ... ... 2/6

and for every £50 above £300 ... ... 5/-

For nominal consideration, or any other not otherwise charged... ... ... 10/-

Transfer of Shares on Cost-book System ... 6d.

Corporations and Companies may compound for transfer duties on payment of 6d. per cent., half-yearly, on paid-up Capital.

Conveyance or transfer—

Bank of England Stock, 7/9 for each transfer.

With regard to the foregoing scale of brokerage, the charges are not exactly uniform amongst all the brokers ; but it will be found in

---

* If the Budget proposals of 29th April, 1909, become law, the rate for stamps on contract notes, where the consideration money is between £5 and £100, will be 6d. instead of 1d.; from £100 to £500, 1/-; from £500 to £1,000, 2/-; with a further 2/- for every additional £1,000.

practice that the variations are very slight, and
that, in the main, they work out very much alike.

At the time of writing, the question of
adopting a uniform scale of commission is
very much to the front, and will shortly be
engaging the special attention of the Stock
Exchange Committee. There is no intention
to prophesy here as to the probable result.

To hark back to the opening remarks made
in this section, it may be well to point out
that the intending investor must not expect
his bankers to *recommend* investments to him.
Bankers are always willing to give any information for the guidance of their customers
regarding any securities they may think of
purchasing, and they will readily obtain from
their brokers a list of securities of which the
brokers have a favourable opinion, or can
recommend, showing the present prices, and
the yield per cent. at such prices.

"Little" holders must not forget that a
similar rule holds good with regard to small
amounts of stock as that which obtains with
regard to small commercial or domestic com-
modities, namely, that best prices are not
always obtainable, and must not therefore be
expected. For example, the seller of £25 of

any railway stock, 5 shares of an American railway, or Rs.500 of an Indian Government security, will probably have to accept a shade less, when disposing of such amounts, than the selling price quoted in the " Stock Exchange Official List."

Where you find it absolutely necessary to give orders for the sale or purchase of securities by telegraph, it is always advisable, if possible, to convey such instructions to London through the medium of your banker, as he employs a code for such purposes. The difficulty that arises, when, instead of taking this course, customers telegraph stock orders to London bankers or brokers direct is, that the receivers of such telegrams have no means of authenticating them. In every case, be sure and follow up your telegraphic message by a confirmatory letter as speedily as possible.

The subject of transfers, so closely connected with investment matters, is specially dealt with under a separate section. The same remark also applies to "Dividends" and " New Issues."

It may not, perhaps, be out of place to remark that, where the customer acts as custodian of his own securities, or securities belonging to others, care should be taken, not only of "bearer" bonds—which cannot, of course, be replaced if lost or destroyed—but also of certificates of registered stocks and shares. This last necessity does not always seem to be readily appreciated, judging by the light way in which applications are sometimes made for duplicate certificates, evidently under the impression that the loss does not matter very much. The applicant might, however, find himself in the position of being informed that he would require to get an indemnity from some approved Guarantee Society before a duplicate certificate would be issued ; and for such an indemnity a charge would be made by the Society, probably at a percentage of the value of the security represented by the certificate.

When giving orders for the purchase of stocks or shares of any kind whatever, while such purchases may be on behalf of trustees, it is useless for you to request that they should be registered in the names of the trustees, *as such*. If the purchase is made for John Jones and Edward Brown, who are Trustees of Richard Robinson, only the names, addresses, and descriptions of Jones and Brown require to be furnished. It may probably be safe to assert that scarcely any Registrar would allow the addition of "Trustees of Richard Robinson," excepting, perhaps, in the case of some of the Trustee Stocks, to appear in a Stock Account.

In concluding this section, the writer would take the liberty of suggesting to the ordinary investor who has spread his money over various securities that it would considerably facilitate matters, both for himself and for others, if he (or she, for ladies would perhaps find it particularly helpful) were to keep an investment card somewhat on the lines of the specimen given at the end of this paragraph. A sheet of foolscap ruled in accordance with it will readily answer the purpose; or, for those who prefer it, investment cards can be purchased, being probably most readily obtainable through special Stock Exchange or bankers' stationers. It has the advantage of showing at a glance the price and actual cost of each investment, the dates on which dividends become due, and dates when drawings take place in respect of bearer bonds, so that the* possessor of such a card should always know exactly how and where he stands both as regards capital and interest. In the matter of investments, as in so many other concerns, method counts for very much.

Amount. £	Name of Investment.	Bought at.	Cost. £ s. d.	Sold at.	Proceeds. £ s. d.	Drawings in.	Dividends.			
							Due.	Amount (gross) £ s. d.	Due.	Amount (gross) £ s. d.
500	Rhodesia Railways 5 % Debentures...	86	431 6 0				1 May	12 10 0	1 Nov.	12 10 0
300	Egyptian Irrigation 4 % Trust ..	102	306 16 0			June & Dec.	1 Jan.	6 0 0	1 July	6 0 0

(A useful card, similar to the above specimen form, called "My Investment Card," is published at 6d. by Messrs. J. A. Byerley and Son, 3, King's Terrace, Southsea, Hants.)

SECTION II.

STOCK EXCHANGE TRANSACTIONS DIRECT WITH BROKERS.

THERE are a great many people, principally in the country, who send orders for the sale or purchase of securities direct to their London brokers; but who, when the question of settling these transactions arrives, request their bankers to complete the matter for them. Possibly from nervous apprehension, or distrust, or some similar cause, they will not part with their securities until a *cash* payment can be received at the actual moment of delivery; and it may be that some similar reason now and again induces the broker to ask the country purchaser to instruct his bankers to hand him *their* draft against his delivery of the securities purchased on account of such customer.

Sometimes there are occasions when a purchaser of bearer securities will carry through the entire transaction direct with his broker up to the point of such broker actually sending him the bonds. For some reason or other, however, he prefers that the broker should take the bonds to the London office of his bank in order that the *bank* may forward them to the branch at which he keeps his account. Provided the customer has previously arranged with the local branch manager as to this, there will probably be no difficulty; although it is scarcely fair that the bank, which has made nothing out of the transaction, should be called upon to pay the postage and registration fee, instead of the broker doing so. But where this is done under the impression that the responsibility in case of loss during transmission will rest with the banker, it is well that both customer and broker should clearly understand that the act of transmission is simply done on the bank's part as a matter of courtesy, and that it accepts no responsibility whatever. This remark applies equally where the bank conducts the cash part of the transaction as described in the foregoing paragraphs; and in order that there may be a clear únderstanding as to this, the customer may possibly be required by his banker to sign an indemnity holding the bank harmless against any loss, etc., that may arise in respect of any such transactions.

It is perhaps well to lay stress upon the necessity for a customer to advise a branch manager when he desires the head office to receive bonds, etc., on his account as, in the absence of such advice, the London banker might be justified in refusing to receive and forward the securities. Probably various London banks could tell of securities that have been brought to their office with the request that they should be sent to such and such a branch "because the owner has an account there," or with the innocent- reason "because you have greater facilities for forwarding them than we have"! A case, however, occurred—and possibly the instance is not a solitary one—where a bank discovered that the securities which were thus sought to be entrusted to its care were likely to become the subject of litigation. The bank naturally declined to receive them, and was on its guard on similar subsequent occasions.

To revert to the matter of indemnity above mentioned, a customer may sometimes place the banker and broker in a rather difficult position, if the transaction be a large one, by requiring the bank to deliver certain securities upon the receipt of others from the broker.

The latter may not be able to hand the new securities to the banker until he has either paid the jobber for them or, if merely an exchange transaction, can give him the securities which the banker is holding. Thus it may happen that, in order to get the matter completed, the banker may have to hand over the customer's securities for some hours before he can get their equivalent ; and for such a risk he may fairly require the customer's indemnity to cover him. Some slight misunderstandings that occasionally occur between bankers and brokers over these transactions on the question of the form of payment could readily be avoided if customers would always inform their broker, as explicitly as they do their bankers, that they require payment in cash or banker's draft, and not by broker's cheque, in exchange for their securities.

SECTION III.

TRANSFERS.

It may seem very unnecessary to advise that a purchaser or seller of stocks and shares should never sign a transfer without first reading it through. Experience, however, shows that there are many people who do so, and that, in consequence, errors in the name or address are allowed to pass without correction, and are accordingly reproduced on the stock or share certificate. These documents, in turn, are sometimes put away instead of being returned to be rectified, and years may elapse before the mistake is pointed out. Needless trouble thus arises for want of a little care in the first instance when the transfer was signed.

In executing a transfer, care should be taken to see that the signatures are affixed in the proper place. Not infrequently the witness will spoil the deed by signing his or her name immediately beneath that of the person whose signature he has witnessed, instead of in the allotted space immediately to the left which is clearly indicated on nearly all transfer deeds. If the witness be a female, it will usually be sufficient if she states, on the line marked "occupation,"—"spinster," "married woman," or "widow," as the case may be. If the witness be a clerk or a domestic servant, the occupation should be given as "clerk to," or "domestic servant to,"—(adding the name of employer). Attention to these little matters of detail may often save delay. As "occupation" may possibly still appear as "description" on a few lingering, antiquated transfer forms, ladies who will note the above instructions will not be likely to fall into the error of one of their sex, who wrote against the word "description,"—"tall and fair, with blue eyes."

The old regulation as to non-validity of the witnessing of a wife's signature by her husband, and *vice versâ*, has now disappeared so far as several companies are concerned; but as the rule still holds good for probably the majority of stocks, etc., it is always better to get an independent witness. Again, where a transfer is executed both by the transferor and transferee at the same time, it is advisable that neither of them should sign as witness to the other's signature.

A transfer should always be signed, and returned to the banker or broker who sent it, with as little delay as possible. If it represents a security that has been sold, it must be in the broker's hands within ten days from the "settling day" for which it was sold, otherwise the stock (or shares, as the case may be) is liable to be "bought-in" against the seller.

The seller will frequently find that the amount of the consideration money stated on a transfer differs from that which he will receive. This is owing to sub-sales by the original buyer, and a note will be found on the subject at the foot of the common transfer form. The other footnote that usually appears on all transfers is one to be carefully observed, namely, that when a transfer is executed out of Great Britain, it is advisable that the signatures be attested by His Majesty's consul or vice-consul, a clergyman, magistrate, or some other person holding a public position, as most companies refuse to recognise signatures not so attested.

A point to be specially observed, when signing transfers, is that the names should be signed either in full, or with all the initials. Ladies are apt sometimes to be delinquents in this respect; and while they have given their names in full, as was necessary, for insertion on the transfers, "Margaret Elizabeth Wood," for example, will sign the deed as "Margaret Wood" only.

Sometimes through illness, or on account of the seller or purchaser of stock being blind or illiterate, transfers can only be executed by a mark. In such cases the following clause should be "worked into" the attestation clause:—"Signed, sealed, and delivered by the within-named ——, by affixing his mark thereto, the contents of the within transfer having first been read through and fully explained to him, and perfectly understood by him." Where the deed is executed by an illiterate person, the witness should be of some standing—say a solicitor, bank manager, etc.; if by someone who is ill, the witness should preferably be a doctor, clergyman, or solicitor.

The usual fee charged by a company for registering a transfer of stock or shares is 2s. 6d., such fee being charged to the purchaser on the contract note. The fee, however, varies with some few companies.

From about a fortnight to a month is the time generally taken for the registration of a transfer. When a certificate has not been received, say, by a month after the transfer was signed, the purchaser should make enquiry for it.

It is an error to assume that the certification of a deed of transfer implies of necessity that it will be registered when lodged for that purpose. The certification clause is of value only as an evidence to the buyer that the certificate has been deposited by the seller, or his broker, at the office of the company whose stock or shares are conveyed on the transfer. Just occasionally it happens that a distringas, or stop, has been placed on the stock or shares intended to be conveyed, and the transfer consequently cannot be registered until such stop has been removed. This consideration, however, need never trouble the purchaser, since the broker who bought for him would have to obtain delivery of stock. from some other quarter if the transfer were completely barred from registration.

When a nominal consideration (such as 5s. or 10s.) is stated on a transfer deed, implying that no money has passed in the transaction, the reason for such nominal consideration should either be endorsed on the transfer or stated in the letter which accompanies it.

A word should be said here in explanation of what are commonly known as "transfer notices." It is a practice with all companies, whose stocks or shares are transferable by deed, to send a notice to the seller or transferor of such stock or shares when the deed purporting to be signed by such seller or transferor is handed to the company for certification, or else when it is lodged with them, together with the certificate, for registration. This, of course, is intended to protect such seller or transferor in the event of forgery ; but only in a very few cases does the company require any acknowledgment of such notice, the assumption being that the notice has duly reached the person for whom it was intended. As a further precaution it is a common practice to send these notices in plain envelopes, that is, in envelopes which do not bear the company's name on the back.

SECTION IV.

COUPONS.

In the course of a year an immense amount of labour is performed by banks on behalf of their customers in the shape of the collection of coupons. Besides those coupons which bankers themselves detach from the bonds which they hold, on account of their customers, a very large number are paid in over the counter by other customers; and at certain seasons of the year, notably in January and July, the work thus entailed on the banks is enormous. In some of the large London banks there are special departments for this class of work; and where a bank has a considerable number of branches, it is no light labour to enter up, classify and list the coupons which are remitted by the various branches; while to these there have also to be added the coupons belonging to London customers.

The coupons, when listed, have to be taken round by "walk" clerks to the various agents

H

or banks at whose offices they are payable,
and the tickets or receipts given to them in
exchange have, in turn, to be presented at the
same offices on the dates named thereon, and
exchanged for payments. Such payments are
then advised to the respective branches for the
credit of the various owners, or placed to the
London customers' accounts, as the case may
be.

This brief sketch of the process of collecting
coupons, from the time of their being forwarded
to London to the date when payment is
received, will give some rough idea of the
nature of the work. It may, perhaps, be remarked, in passing, that it is a very unprofitable
department to the banker, seeing that he
receives no remuneration for the services thus
rendered, for which exclusive purpose he is
compelled to employ a certain number of
clerks.

A few notes may possibly be of assistance
under this heading for the guidance of those
who keep their securities in their own possession, or possibly in a box at the bank, and
detach their coupons from time to time :—

(1) Do not fall into the mistake of sending
    your coupons direct to the bank or agent

by whom they are payable, as it is
contrary to their practice to receive them
for collection in this way, and to remit
proceeds by post. The proper course
is to entrust them to your own bankers
for collection on your behalf; or, if you
have no banking account, you should
ask some friend who has one to attend
to the matter for you.

(2) Most coupons are payable on the 1st of
the month, by far the greatest number
falling due on 1st January and 1st July.
As regards these last-named dates,
always let your banker have the coupons
a month before they are due ; as regards
other dates, you should lodge them
with him about a fortnight to three
weeks before they are payable. In cases
where you may require to sell the relative bonds between the time of your
usually detaching the coupons and the
date when they become payable, you
should mention the matter to your
branch manager and he will be able to
advise you as to whether the bonds will
require the coming coupon to be left
attached or otherwise. You may note

that, as a general rule, bonds are quoted "ex dividend" on the Stock Exchange Official List on the date when the coupons are due. Thus, if you sold £100 Queensland 4 per cent. bond on 31st December, the 1st January coupon would have to be attached, as it would be included in the price you would receive for it from the buyer. But if you sold it on 1st January, *you* would be entitled to the coupon, as its value, or an approximate amount thereto, would be deducted from the price quoted that day for the bonds.

(3) It is not advisable to hoard up coupons or to keep them back several months after they become due. While there may be little or no risk of their not being met when presented, the fact of their being kept so long outstanding occasions much trouble to the agents as they are unable to close or settle up their books; while in certain cases, such as Turkish Bonds and South Austrian Railway Obligations, there is an actual danger of coupons that are out of date beyond a certain time being

forfeited. If you are the holder of
Russian Bonds, you should carefully
examine the lists of drawn bonds as
they appear, since it is possible for
coupons to continue to be paid long
after the bonds have been drawn; and
when, perhaps by accident, the drawing
is at length discovered, you have to
accept payment of the bond *less* the
amount of coupons that have been paid
since the date when the bond was repayable.

Of course, where your banker has
the care of your securities and detaches
the coupons for you, you are relieved
of the necessity for noting some of the
foregoing points ; still, as a matter of
interest, it is worth while to know them.
But while bankers will watch lists of
drawn bonds, they decline to accept
responsibility, should a drawing chance
(which is a very rare thing) to escape
their notice.

(4) It should be remembered that bankers
are under an obligation to deduct
income tax before crediting the proceeds
of coupons payable abroad, and the

neglect of this would subject them to a heavy penalty.

(5) When all the coupons attached to your bonds are exhausted, you should hand the bonds to your bank, in order that fresh sheets of coupons may be obtained. Probably, however, you will find what is called a " talon " on the bond, and where this is the case, you should send the " talon " only. When the new talons and coupon sheets are received, they should be carefully *gummed*, not *pinned*, to the bond.

BONDS DRAWN, RENEWED OR CONVERTED.

THERE is a certain amount of laxity among the holders of bonds which are subject to drawings in watching the lists of such drawings from time to time as they are issued. It is an unpleasant experience to receive a coupon back for a half year's interest with the intimation that the bond should have been presented for payment six months previously; but the case is still more serious, where, as has recently been brought home to holders of Russian Bonds, it is possible for years to elapse before the holder of the bond discovers that his bond has been long since drawn for payment, and has the severe shock of receiving the amount of the principal, minus several years' interest payments dating back to the time when the bonds should have been redeemed. Where the bondholder prefers to retain his bond in his own keeping, he should either take in the

Bondholders' Register, which is published fortnightly, and contains lists of the various drawings, or else he should ascertain from his bankers the dates when the drawings of those bonds in which he is interested take place, and then obtain lists of such drawings as and when they are issued. The simpler plan is, of course, to deposit the bonds with the banker, who watches all drawings on behalf of his customers. Should, however, the bank by any chance overlook a bond which has been drawn, they would doubtless claim that they cannot be held responsible for such omission. Seeing that the service rendered is a gratuitous one, this is but fair; and, happily for all concerned, it would appear as though the occasions when such omissions occur are extremely rare.

The same instructions with regard to the presentation of drawn or matured bonds hold good as in the case of coupons, namely, that they must not be sent for collection to the bankers or agents at whose offices they are payable, as it is contrary to practice for payments to be made by postal remittance. The bonds should therefore be entrusted to your own banker for collection on your behalf.

Where foreign bonds (*e.g.,* American Railway, Japanese Exchequer, etc., etc.) have
been drawn, payment can be obtained by
selling them in London "with recourse" (*i.e.,*
the customer must hand the proceeds back to
the bank if the bonds should be returned for
any reason) ; or the bonds can be sent out to
the countries where payable, and the amount
credited to the customer when received by
the bank.

Bonds for Renewal.—When all the coupons
on a bond have become exhausted a fresh
sheet of coupons must be obtained, and for
this purpose it will usually be found that a
slip called a "talon" is attached to the bond.
In almost every case it will be sufficient if this
slip is detached and sent to your banker, who
will then obtain the further supply of coupons
for you. It may, however, be several weeks
before the new coupons reach you. Should
your bonds be in the bank's keeping, you need
not trouble about the matter as the bank will
attend to it for you.

Conversion of Bonds.—Some years ago it
was not an infrequent operation for bonds of
any description to be exchanged for others

bearing a lower rate of interest. Such operations, however, are now only very occasional.

All such matters are usually well advertised ; but here again, as in the case of bonds requiring new coupon sheets, your banker will attend to the matter as regards bonds held on your account, and will communicate with you for the purpose of getting your instructions.

NEW ISSUES, APPLICATIONS FOR, ETC.

WHEN sending in an application for stocks or shares of some new loan that is advertised, you will find that you are usually required to send payment of 5 per cent. or 10 per cent. with your application. For the guidance of some it is necessary to point out that such payment must be on the nominal amount of stock applied for, and must not be calculated on the issue price, supposing such price to be below or above par. That is to say, if you are applying for £100 of the Blanktown Corporation 3 per cent. stock, which is being issued at 90 per cent., you must send, if the payment required on application is 5 per cent., a remittance for £5, not £4 10s.

Always make a note in your diary of the dates when the remaining instalments become

due, and see that they are paid with the
promptitude with which it would be necessary
for you to meet your acceptance on the date
of its maturity. There is considerable laxity
—though it is frequently unintentional—on
the part of many who subscribe to new issues,
in paying the instalments by the proper dates.
While the usual clause in a prospectus as to
forfeiture if instalments are not paid by the
fixed dates is very rarely put in force, bankers
have frequently no alternative but to charge
interest at 5 per cent. or more on overdue
instalments. Where, as frequently happens,
the first dividend payment is calculated from
the actual due date of each instalment, it is
obviously unfair that an allottee should keep
the company out of its money for several
days ; and the only recourse is, therefore, for
the company to impose a fine upon such
allottee in the shape of an interest charge as
above mentioned.

Always note to send your allotment letter
or scrip *with* the payment of each instalment.
If you are resident in a provincial town the
manager of your bank will always be pleased
to forward these to his London agent or head
office for you ; and upon your giving him

written instructions to such effect he will see to the payment of all instalments as they become due, and to the subsequent exchange of provisional documents for the definitive securities. In fact your banker can send in the original application, if you so desire ; and where time and speed are an object—such as in the case of a popular issue for which the list may only remain open a few hours—you can scarcely do better than intrust the matter to him, as he can at once telegraph on your behalf to his head office (supposing the issue to be made in London) with the advantage of a private code which ensures the genuineness of the telegram. For in applications for new issues, as well as in giving instructions for the sale or purchase of stocks, it is usually inadvisable for a private individual to send orders by wire, as the receiver has no means of authenticating the telegrams.

Where the holder of fully-paid allotment letters or scrip relating to *registered* stock or shares of some company prefers to effect their exchange himself, rather than through his banker, or because he has no banking account, he must bear in mind that it is to the secretary of such company, and not to the bank to whom he paid the instalments, that he must send the documents to be exchanged. Care must be taken that all receipts are forwarded. Where, however, the definitive securities to be received in exchange for allotment letter or scrip are in "bearer" form, that is to say in the shape of bonds, it is advisable to hand such allotment letters or scrip certificates to your bankers, as the agents in London, through whom the issue was made, will not be responsible for the safe delivery of bonds sent by post to a private individual.

Another point to be noted is, that where you send in your application, or pay an instalment, direct, the accompanying remittance should be either a cheque payable to bearer, or banknotes. There are some, however, though happily but few, who will send a miscellaneous collection of cheques, dividend warrants, etc., to pay the sum due on application or allotment, or for the amount of an instalment, forgetful of the fact that such articles should properly be paid in to their account with their own bankers. Frequently the address of the allottee does not appear on his allotment letter ; where such is the case, the allottee, when remitting further payment, should always enclose a slip giving the address to which the receipt is to be forwarded.

Needless correspondence and trouble might sometimes be avoided by a careful perusal of the prospectus, and by noting the dates when payments are to be made, and the allotment letters to be exchanged for scrip certificates or other security.

Be careful not to write your name on scrip certificates or bonds, or on any kind of " bearer " securities, as such a practice renders them liable to be " bad delivery " on the Stock Exchange.

Ladies should take special note of the request on the application form, to state whether " Mrs." or " Miss." When your scrip has been fully paid, if no date is mentioned therein as to when it will be exchangeable for definitive securities, you should write and ascertain the necessary information on this point. Unfortunately, there are some who will retain their scrip for months, or even years, the issuing agents in the meantime holding bonds with the various overdue coupons attached, and possibly being without any means of tracing who is holding the relative scrip.

SECTION VII.

FRACTIONS AND "RIGHTS."

IT often happens in conversion operations, whether of Foreign Bonds, American Railway Shares or other securities, as also in the issue *pro ratâ* of new capital of an existing concern, that fractions result; and such fractions can usually be sold outright, or further fractions purchased to make up a whole number or amount. It is well to bear in mind that these fractions should always be dealt with at an early date; for while there may occasionally be no time limit for such dealings mentioned thereon, the natural tendency is for the bulk of them to be dealt with speedily, and consequently the few that are left long outstanding become unmarketable, and therefore valueless.

These remarks apply equally in the case of "rights" in so far as such "rights" are fractional, or require to be dealt with during a specified period. "Rights" may of course take various forms, such as subscription warrants, offers of allotment, allotment letters with renunciation forms, etc.

SECTION VIII.

"EX DIVIDEND."

IT frequently happens, especially at the close of each half year, that bonds and stocks are sold or purchased "ex dividend"; an arrangement which seems to puzzle many. It may be safe to state, as a general rule, that so far as bonds with coupons attached are concerned, such bonds are marked on the Stock Exchange Official List "Ex Dividend" (or, more correctly, "Ex Coupon") on the evening of the date when the coupon becomes payable. For example, as already mentioned elsewhere, if you bouɡ ɪt £100 Queensland 4 per cent. bonds on the 31st December you would be entitled to the 1st January coupon; and your broker who purchased the bond would see to it that, if for any reason the coupon had been detached, you received the full amount ,of such coupon in lieu of the actual document.

On the other hand there are some who forget that when, to use the above illustration, they sell such bond on the 31st December they obtain the amount of the coupon in the price they receive for the bond. They take it as a matter of course that, as they will not be paid for the bond until the mid-January settling day, they are entitled to the coupon as well. Such persons require to remember that they cannot eat their cake and have it too.

Government and Colonial Stocks, the dividends on which are payable at the Bank of England, are usually marked " Ex Dividend " about four or five weeks before such dividends are due. For example, Consols on which dividends are payable 5th January, April, July and October are marked " Ex Dividend " between the 1st and 3rd December, March, June and September respectively.

For the generality of Stocks and Shares the rule is to mark them " Ex Dividend " on the official list on the settling day next succeeding the date when the dividends are payable. If therefore you have sold, say £100 Midland Railway Preferred Converted Ordinary Stock for the end of August account, and your dividend reaches you, say on the 21st or 22nd of August, you will require to surrender that dividend, seeing that it is included in the price you have received for the stock.

Yet another rule that obtains with regard to the " Ex Dividend " marking in the " Stock Exchange Official List," may perhaps best be explained by the following illustration:— Where a bank, for example, declares a dividend, and such declaration does not require to be confirmed at the general meeting of its shareholders, the shares would be quoted " Ex Dividend" at the settlement next after such declaration, although the general meeting might not then have been held. If, however, the sanction of the general meeting of shareholders has to be obtained, the shares would not be quoted " Ex Dividend" until after such confirmation.

It is very general for brokers, when selling stocks or shares " Ex Dividend," to mark the contract note to that effect, so that the seller or buyer need not be in any doubt upon the point. Where the matter sometimes becomes a little complicated is in cases where stocks and shares have been purchased " Cum Dividend," but too late for the transfer to be lodged at the office of the company in time for registration before the dividends are sent out. In this case the amount of dividend has to be claimed from the brokers of the seller.

A difficulty arises where the purchaser wishes to recover income tax, seeing that it is not very easy to obtain either the upper half of the dividend warrant, or a duplicate, for the purpose of claiming such tax. Moreover, if such documents were obtained it would be the *seller's* name that would appear thereon, and the buyer would have to prove his claim to the thorough satisfaction of the Inland Revenue authorities before he could recover the tax. This difficulty has, however, been solved, within a comparatively recent period, by stockbrokers themselves giving the required certificate as to the deduction of income tax; and these certificates are accepted by the Inland Revenue authorities.

SECTION IX.

PROVING DEATH (GENERAL).

A special section has already been devoted to the subject of proving death as far as the Bank of England is concerned. As regards other banks, and the vast number of miscellaneous companies, regulations, of course, vary. They may be summarised briefly as follows :—

(1) Where stocks or shares stand in the sole name of the deceased, or where the deceased is the last survivor in a joint account, either probate or letters of administration will be required.

(2) Where the deceased was the holder in a joint account, in which there is at least one survivor, several companies will probably be satisfied with the production of the certificate of death issued by the district registry, on the back of which they will make a note that it has been exhibited. Other companies, however, require a copy to retain; while some of the banks will only accept a

death certificate when issued by Somerset House, or by the Chief Registry in Edinburgh or Dublin; such death certificate to be supported, where required, by a declaration of comparison and identity, both documents being retained by the bank.

(3) Certified burial extracts are also accepted by some institutions, and these again are usually required to be accompanied by a declaration of comparison and identity.

On the books of some companies, as at the Bank of England, the stock remains in the name of a deceased person; and when the death of the executors takes place, on the usual proof being lodged at the bank the stock will be at the disposal of the executors of the last surviving executor. But if the said last surviving executor should die intestate, the administrator cannot act, nor can executors of an administrator be recognised. A grant *de bonis non* will, in these cases, have to be taken out and exhibited.

On the other hand, several companies, especially those where there is a liability attaching to the shares, require the shares to be transferred out of the name of the deceased person, either by sale, or else by transfer (special or otherwise) to the executors as individual holders. In such instances, the next accruing dividend after the death of the shareholder has been proved may possibly be retained until the shares have been transferred.

As regards current accounts, deposit accounts, or deposit receipts standing in the sole name of the deceased, either probate of will or letters of administration must of necessity be lodged at his bankers to prove death thereon.

In the course of a year a London bank receives from its various branches a large number of probates, death and burial certificates, etc., with the request to prove the death of the various persons therein referred to, at the offices of sundry banks and companies. These should always be accompanied by the stock or share certificates, with any outstanding dividend warrants, in respect of which death is to be proved. While all companies do not insist on the production of the stock or share certificates, it is nevertheless the better plan to exhibit them and have them marked with a note as to the death, for it saves doubt on the point, and possible delay and trouble later on.

It is perhaps not too much to state that there are few who have a more intimate knowledge of, and practical acquaintance with, the many technicalities and requirements connected with the matter of "proving death" than some of our bank managers and the officials in the London banks upon whom this particular class of work devolves.

SECTION X.

MARRIAGE (ALTERATION OF NAME, ETC., ON).

THERE are various regulations with regard to the alteration on the books of a bank or company of the name of a female stockholder or shareholder on her marriage. Several institutions require simply the lodgment of a request signed by her, both in her old and new names, stating the name in full of her husband, her new address, and the accounts in which it is desired to have the alteration made. Perhaps, however, in the majority of cases the certificate of marriage is required, the company returning it after they have endorsed a note thereon as to its entry in their books. It is desirable that the stock or share certificate should always accompany the request form or marriage certificate, as either a note will be made thereon or a new certificate will be issued in exchange. Again, several companies are satisfied with the description "married

woman," while others require " wife of————"
to be stated, when stock is bought or sold ; to
be on the safe side, therefore, it is perhaps as
well always to give the latter description.
Any dividend warrants, also, that may have
been sent to the stockholder in her maiden
name, but subsequent to her marriage, should
be forwarded with the above-mentioned
documents in order that the necessary alteration
may be made thereon.

SECTION XI.

DISTRINGASES, STOPS, LIENS.

WHERE it is desired to prevent the sale or transfer of stocks or shares, presumably because of some personal interest therein, various courses are adopted according to the nature or place of registration of such securities. As regards stocks inscribed at the Bank of England, the custom is to place what is termed a "distringas" or "stop" upon the stock; and all communications, whether for imposing or removing such "stops," have to pass through Messrs. Freshfield, of 31, Old Jewry, E.C., who are the Bank of England's solicitors. Eight days' notice is required to be given for the withdrawal of a "distringas." Forms for affidavit and notice can be purchased from Waterlow and Sons Limited, London Wall, E.C., and other law stationers; but probably for the most part "distringases" are lodged through the medium of solicitors, instead of by private individuals on their own account.

Sometimes a case arises, where, for example, the manager of the Croydon and Norwood Banking Company advises the Cornhill and Leadenhall Bank that their shareholder, Mr. Thomas Brown, has deposited with them his certificate of ten shares in that bank as security against a loan. The customary course in such cases is, for the Cornhill and Leadenhall Bank to reply that they cannot accept service of such notice, and that in order to perfect their security the Croydon and Norwood Bank should obtain Mr. Brown's transference of the shares into the names of their nominees. The Cornhill and Leadenhall Bank would, nevertheless, probably make a note of the matter in their Registers, and would advise the Croydon and Norwood Bank when it was sought to transfer the shares. At the same time it is possibly open to doubt as to whether such notice can be held to be binding; and no doubt the proper course, when a loan is made, whether against bank shares or other registered securities, is for such shares or stocks to be transferred, whenever practicable, into the names of the person, firm, company, bank or its nominees, by whom the advance is made.

Sometimes a solicitor or private individual wishes to know whether there is any distringas or stop against any particular stock or shares. Before, however, the bank or company at whose offices the books are kept answer the enquiry, they will require an authority from the stockholder, or one of the stockholders if a joint account, to give the information that is sought for.

It is, of course, possible for there to be more than one distringas on an account.

As a rule, the payment of dividends is not interfered with by a distringas or notice of lien.

Now and again application is made to the Bank of England for a power of attorney for sale, or a transfer deed is presented to a Bank, before a distringas has been removed. In the first-named case the application form would be returned unless the applicant specially stated thereon "pending removal of distringas"; and the power cannot be acted upon until the expiry of eight days' notice which, in this instance, would be calculated from the date when the application was lodged. Similarly, the person presenting a transfer for registration would be informed by the banker that the stock represented by it could not be transferred until the expiry of the requisite period in regard to the notice which he (the banker) would be sending forthwith to the person or firm who placed the distringas on the account.

SECTION XII.

SECURITIES, DEEDS, BOXES, Etc., FOR SAFE CUSTODY.

Your bankers will at all times be ready to take charge of securities on your behalf, either

(1) as a sealed parcel, to be opened only by yourself or on your authority; or

(2) in your own box, to which you can obtain access at any time during banking hours; or

(3) they will enter the various securities in your name in their registers, detaching and collecting coupons for you, if you so desire, and also receiving dividends in respect of inscribed stocks, or registered stocks and shares. For the purpose of receiving dividends on such registered securities on your behalf they will supply you with all request forms as required by the various companies.

Where your securities are lodged in the manner described in case (3) above, you have

the additional advantage, supposing you hold
bearer bonds subject to drawings, of the bank
watching the advertisements of drawn bonds
as they are published from time to time.
The bank notifies its customers when any of
their bonds are drawn ; at the same time, the
customer must remember, as previously
remarked, that he cannot hold his banker
responsible, should a drawing escape his
attention. If you are the holder of any
bearer bonds subject to drawings, it would
be well for you to keep a note before you of
the date when such drawings take place, in
order that you may give a reminder to your
banker. In all probability he will already
have a note of the matter before him, and he
himself will scan the list of drawings for you.
Still, this reminder on your part will help to
make assurance doubly sure, and to save you
from the annoyance of not discovering that
your bond has been drawn until the next half-
yearly coupon is returned to you unpaid, with
a note that the bond should have been collected
six months previously. Where securities,
boxes, or parcels of any kind are deposited
with a bank in more than one name, the bank
must be furnished with specimen signatures of

all parties ; and the instructions as to dealing with such securities, etc., must be clear and explicit.

The boxes, which are lodged in a bank's strong room for the convenience of various customers, are generally increased in number during the summer months, when plate chests and similar boxes containing valuables are handed over to them for safe custody during the holiday season. Some bankers—possibly most bankers—decline to give receipts for such boxes, or indeed receipts for any securities that may be lodged with them, whether for safe custody or otherwise, for the obvious reason that such receipts might easily get into the wrong hands. They will, however, always write you a memorandum or a letter to the effect that such and such securities or boxes have been lodged with them on your behalf. Such letter, of course, is simply a formal communication for your own satisfaction ; and it has the great advantage of being useless to anyone who might seek to obtain in a fraudulent way, as he *might* be able to do in exchange for a receipt, the securities, etc., to which it refers. Specific instructions must always be given whenever you desire that any person or persons

K

other than yourself should have access to your box, and specimen signatures of such person or persons must be supplied to the bank. Similar precautions must be observed if and when you wish to remove the box from the bank.

CHAPTER V.

DIVIDENDS, Etc.

DIVIDEND REQUEST FORMS AND AUTHORITIES.

IT is becoming increasingly the custom for holders of stocks or shares of any kind to give instructions to the bank, firm, or agent, by whom the dividends are paid, to forward such dividends to their bankers as and when they become due. For such purpose it is necessary that the stockholder or, if more than one in an account, *all* the holders, should sign a form of request for dividends to be so forwarded. Special forms are usually required, and can be readily obtained from the bank or company that pays the dividends. Sometimes the stockholder will merely send a written request with regard to his dividends; provided it be properly worded it will possibly be accepted, but it not infrequently happens that such letters fail of their purpose, either on account of their being restrictive, or through their being in other respects imperfect or incomplete. For instance, a stockholder who makes his request by letter is very apt to ask that the dividends on a *definite* amount of Stock may be sent to his bankers; overlooking that, in the event of the stock being increased at any time, his request would be thereby practically invalid. His instructions *ought* to state "Dividends on the amount now or at any future time standing in my name." For other reasons, however, it is preferable to take the little extra trouble to procure the proper forms applicable to the stocks or shares in question.

When the form is completed it should be sent to the bank, firm, or agent, to whom it is addressed, *through the banker to whom the dividends are to be paid,* in order that the latter may enter it in his register. Your banker, if in the country, will then forward it to his head office, presuming the books of the stocks or shares in question are kept in London; and the head office will also make an entry of the form, in order that when the dividends, accompanied probably by several others of the same sort, are paid to them, they may know to what branch the amounts are to be advised. Sometimes, however, the stockholder makes the mistake of sending in his dividend request *direct* to the bank or company whose shares or stock he holds; consequently his own banker has no knowledge of the matter; and thus, by way of illustration, the Universal Bank in London may receive a dividend for £10 in favour of John Jones amongst dozens of others from the London & North Western Railway, and it is not until after enquiry from the railway company that the bank learn that the warrant has been forwarded to them under instructions from Mr. John Jones, of 34, Nonsuch Road, Liverpool; they then find that he has an account with their Liverpool Branch, and advise the amount there accordingly.

It may here be stated that, as a matter of general practice, the Bank of England will not forward dividends to a country bank which has a head office in London, but require such head office to claim from them all dividends payable under authorities in their favour given by the customers, both of their London and country branches. Thus it comes about that it is the London address of your banker, and not that of your particular branch, which requires to be filled in on all Bank of England dividend request forms. The larger railway companies also, as a rule, follow the practice of the Bank of England as regards the payment of all dividends to the London head office of a bank instead of to the various branches. All other bankers and companies, however, with probably very few exceptions, will forward dividend warrants direct to any branch of a bank, and can therefore be instructed accordingly.

Sometimes a stockholder, when filling in a form of request for dividends to be sent to his banker, will add "For the credit of my account"; or, in a joint account, the stockholders will similarly add "For credit of such and such an account." Most banks, however, including the Bank of England, will ignore any such additional instructions; in fact a note appears on several request forms stating that the bank will not undertake to cross the dividend warrant to any particular banker, nor to forward the dividend to the credit of any particular account. The instructions as to the disposal of the warrants should be given to *your own* banker, somewhat in the following terms :—

Address...

Date..19

To THE UNIVERSAL BANK, LIMITED, LIVERPOOL.

Please place the dividends as and when received by you on any $\frac{\text{amount of}}{\text{number of}}$ ....$\frac{\text{Stock}}{\text{Shares}}$ now or at any future time standing in $\frac{\text{my sole}}{\text{our joint}}$ name(s) to the credit of..... .... at your Office.

(Signed)............ ....

....

....

The present amount of the stock, or the existing number of shares held, can be stated at the *foot* of the form; or if there be a long list of securities they can be scheduled at the *back* of the above authority, the existing amount in each case being added in parentheses *after* the name of the stock. In the blank space in the *above* form between $\frac{\text{amount of}}{\text{number of}}$ and $\frac{\text{Stock}}{\text{Shares}}$ the phrase " as per list at back " can be filled in, and such list or schedule, as well as the front of the form, should be signed by *all* the stockholders.

Perhaps it may be well to note, in passing, that where you give instructions for the payment of dividends to your banker, such instructions should simply give the name and address of the bank, and not of an official therein, whether by name or otherwise.

It has been sought, as far as possible, to limit the remarks under this heading strictly to the execution of requests and authorities relating to dividends, a separate section being devoted to the actual subject of Dividend Warrants. The two subjects, however, dovetail into each other, and must be read or studied together.

Special request forms for Chancery Dividend payments to be remitted to bankers are required where it is desired that bankers shall collect such dividends.

SECTION II.

DIVIDENDS (GENERAL).

IT is now an almost universal practice to forward by post dividends on all stocks and shares to the proprietor in whose name they are registered, to the first-named holder in a joint account, and to the first executor of a deceased holder. Dividend warrants on joint accounts are made out, in a general way, "Pay James Brown and another," "Pay John Bull and others." Only the first-named person, however, on the account need discharge the warrant. It should scarcely be necessary to state, but there are nevertheless some who need a reminder, that it is not wise to hoard up dividend warrants. When they are allowed to accumulate they become, after a certain time, "out of date"; and before they can be paid they require to be returned to the bank or company by whom they were originally issued, in order that they may be marked for payment. The non-presentation of the warrants within a reasonable time after their issue is, moreover, troublesome to the bank or company which sent them out, as they are unable to close their books because of the outstanding amount.

As regards dividends on bank shares, holders should bear in mind that, in a large number of cases, there is no fixed day of the month for their payment. The large banks have some thousands of shareholders on their books, and they cannot know at what rate the dividend will be paid until the half-year has closed. The dividends are usually paid round about the same dates year by year. This subject is, however, more fully dealt with under the heading of " Bank Shares and Dividends thereon." Of course, in cases where "fixed" rates of interest are payable, such as on government, colonial, corporation, and other stocks, it is the custom for there to be a fixed date of payment.

In the section "Dividend Request Forms" we have referred to the practice of dividends being received by bankers on behalf of their customers. It may be as well, however, to give a reminder here that, while bankers readily undertake to receive such dividends, they are not responsible for seeing that these dividends

are regularly paid to them. A little reflection
will show that this is but reasonable, since,
for example, John Jones, who has received
dividends on his Midland Railway Debenture
Stock through his bankers, may sell the stock
through his brokers without mentioning the
matter to his bankers; and the latter cannot,
of course, be expected to write to John Jones
and enquire why no dividend has been received
on his account. There is, however, one excep-
tion with regard to this matter of the receipt
of dividends, namely, in regard to stocks inscribed at the Bank of England. Where a
holder of these sells or buys any stock otherwise than through his bankers, he should
always advise them of the change, as the Bank
of England will alter the amount of stock on
the list sent in by the banker who collects the
dividends, and will require from him confirmation of such alteration.

Nearly every half-year witnesses a certain
number of dividends returned through the post
from a variety of causes, chiefly from change of
address of the shareholder; or, if in the summer-
time, through his absence from home. To
guard against this last-named contingency, it
is always advisable, before going away, to

address a letter to the bank or company, asking them to forward the dividend next due on the stock or shares held (giving particulars) to such and such an address, pointing out that the request only applies to the forthcoming dividend. This small precaution will probably save a great deal of trouble, and will prevent the dividend from getting lost.

SECTION III.

BANK SHARES AND DIVIDENDS THEREON.

As this work is intended especially for those who are customers of banks, and holders of bank shares, it is only fitting that a special section should be devoted to the above subject; and it is hoped that the table given at the end of this chapter, showing the approximate dates on which most of the large London and country banks pay their dividends, will prove of special service. It is impossible, within the compass of this small volume, to give a complete list of banks; but the subjoined list will be found to contain most of the large institutions in which British investors are interested. Reference to it from time to time may obviate the necessity of writing to enquire when the dividend is likely to be paid. As is well known, it is customary for the books to be closed for a certain period for the preparation of the dividend warrants,—a circumstance which brings to mind an amusing letter the writer once saw from a shareholder to the following effect: "As I have no notice of the closing of your bank I am feeling anxious to know when I am likely to receive my half-yearly dividend warrant."

As in other matters, so also in regard to the holding of bank shares, it needs to be reiterated that banks will not accept notice of trust, nor register trustees as such. Sometimes it is sought to open more than one account by reversing the order of names, but it is perhaps safe to say that, where discovered, this will not be allowed. It may be argued that the Bank of England will allow as many as four accounts in Consols or other stocks; but the case is not on "all fours" with a bank where a liability exists in respect of its capital.

Bank shares may not be held by, nor registered in the name of, a person under age.

It is unnecessary to acknowledge the receipt of dividend warrants.

Dividend warrants should always be discharged by the person in whose favour they are made out; sometimes, however, a shareholder will allow someone else to sign his (the shareholder's) name on the warrant. This is apt to lead to trouble and confusion where reference has to be made to the signature for comparison or verification.

For proof of marriage a female stockholder should send her marriage certificate, together with the share certificate, to the bank. The former will be returned to her after a note has been made on the bank's register, and a new share certificate will be sent to her.

As regards proving death of a holder of bank shares, either the probate or the letters of administration must always be sent where the shares stood in the deceased holder's sole name; while a death certificate or certified burial extract, with or without a declaration of identity, etc., will probably suffice where the deceased was the holder in a joint account. Some banks will send out one dividend after the death has been proved, but will retain subsequent dividends until the shares have either been sold, or otherwise transferred out of the deceased holder's name. A note of their requirements is enclosed by most banks in the probate, when returning it after it has been registered on their books.

L

It is doubtless well known that the bank's register of members can be inspected during business hours upon payment of one shilling.

All changes of address, immediately they occur, should be notified to the secretary of the bank. The necessity for this requires, perhaps, to be specially borne in mind by that class of shareholders who are most apt to forget it, *viz.*, those by whose instructions dividends are sent to their bankers.

NAME.	Dividends due in, on, or about	
Anglo-South American Bank, Limited .	End April	End Oct.
Bank of Africa, Limited	End Mch.	End Oct.
Bank of Australasia	March	Sept.
Bank of British North America . .	2 April	1 Oct.
Bank of England	5 April	5 Oct.
Bank of Ireland	1 Feb.	1 Aug.
Bank of Liverpool, Limited . . .	Mid. Jan.	Mid. July
Bank of Scotland	Mid. April	Mid. Oct.
Barclay & Co., Limited	1 Feb.	1 Aug.
Belfast Banking Co., Limited . . .	15 Feb.	15 Aug.
British Linen Bank	Mid. Mch.	Mid. Sept.
Canadian Bank of Commerce . . .	1 March 1 Sept.	1 June 1 Dec.
Capital and Counties Bank, Limited .	Mid. Jan.	End July
Chartered Bank of India, Australia and China	Mid. April	Mid. Oct.
Clydesdale Bank, Limited . . .	Mid. Feb.	Early Aug.
Colonial Bank	Mid April	Mid. Oct.
Commercial Bank of Scotland, Limited .	Jan.	July
Crompton & Evans Union Bank, Limited .	1 Feb.	1 Aug.
Halifax Joint Stock Banking Co., Limited	Early Feb.	Early Aug.
Hibernian Bank, Limited	Early Feb.	Early Aug.
Hong Kong & Shanghai Banking Corporation	Feb.	Aug.
Lancashire and Yorkshire Bank, Limited	End Jan.	July
Lloyds Bank, Limited	End Jan.	July
London & Brazilian Bank, Limited . .	End April	End Oct.

NAME.	Dividends due in, on, or about.	
London & County Banking Co., Limited	17 Feb.	1 Aug.
London & Provincial Bank, Limited	3rd wk. in Jan.	3rd wk. in July
London & River Plate Bank, Limited	Mid. June	Mid. Dec.
London & South Western Bank, Limited	Feb.	6 Aug.
London & Westminster Bank, Limited	End Jan.	End July
London City & Midland Bank, Limited	1 Feb.	1 Aug.
London Joint Stock Bank, Limited	Mid. Jan.	Mid. July
Manchester and County Bank, Limited	End Jan.	End July
Manchester & Liverpool District Banking Co., Limited	Mid. Jan.	Mid. July
Martin's Bank, Limited	End Feb.	End Aug.
Metropolitan Bank (of England and Wales), Limited	1 Feb.	1 Aug.
Munster & Leinster Bank, Limited	End Jan.	End July
National Bank, Limited	End Jan.	End July
National Bank of India, Limited	End Mch.	End Sept.
National Bank of Scotland, Limited	2nd Tuesday in Jan. and	July
National Discount Co., Limited	End Jan.	Mid. July
National Provincial Bank of England, Limited	EarlyFeb.	EarlyAug.
North of Scotland & Town & County Bank, Limited	May	Nov.
Northamptonshire Union Bank, Limited	Feb.	Aug.
North Eastern Banking Co., Limited	End Jan.	End July
Northern Banking Co., Limited	10 Mch.	10 Sept.
Parr's Bank, Limited	3 Feb.	7 Aug.
Provincial Bank of Ireland, Limited	1 Feb.	1 Aug.
Royal Bank of Ireland, Limited	April	Oct.
Royal Bank of Scotland	Midsummer	Christmas
Stamford, Spalding & Boston Banking Co., Limited	Feb.	Aug.
Standard Bank of South Africa, Limited	Mid.April	Mid. Oct.
Stuckey's Banking Co., Limited	End Jan.	End July
Ulster Bank, Limited	15 March	15 Sept.
Union Bank of Australia, Limited	End Jan.	22 July
Union Bank of Manchester, Limited	Mid. Jan.	Mid. July
Union Bank of Scotland, Limited	10 May	10 Nov.
Union Discount Co. of London, Limited	18 Jan.	18 July
Union of London & Smiths Bank, Limited	End Jan.	End July
United Counties Bank, Limited	1 Feb.	1 Aug.
Williams Deacon's Bank, Limited	End Jan.	End July
Wilts & Dorset Banking Co., Limited	Early Jan.	Early July

CHAPTER VI.

MISCELLANEOUS.

CORRESPONDENCE.

IT has been the writer's special aim to make this work a standard guide book for every class of bank customer. Whether the reader be a lady, professional man, tradesman or a person of independent means, he or she will, it is hoped, find all enquiries answered, difficulties met, and problems solved on whatever relates to their personal transactions, in these pages. Since several of the matters dealt with must, of necessity, form the subject of correspondence, a brief section under this heading may be found helpful.

To those who carp at what they are wont to look upon as the big profits made by a bank, it may not be out of place to mention here what a very large unremunerative outlay a bank has to make in some of its departments. For instance, as regards the collection of coupons, the head office, or London agents, of the country banks have to employ a staff of clerks engaged on this work alone, and for these . services the bank receives nothing whatever from its customers. The stationery bill of a large bank, not forgetting the expensive item of cheques for which the customer only pays the stamp duty thereon impressed, is enormous; while under this particular heading of correspondence, the expenses of postage in a large bank in the course of a year run into thousands of pounds. These may be seemingly small points, but they are nevertheless interesting, and may give food for reflection to those who are accustomed to look upon banks merely as profit-making machines.

Where a customer keeps his account at a country branch, no question arises as to whom the correspondence should be addressed, for naturally all communications on the subject of his account are sent to the manager. The case, however, is somewhat different as regards correspondence with a London bank, where, in addition to the manager, there are also the general managers, chief inspector, secretary, and other officials. As a rule, it may be safely taken that correspondence relating to branch matters should be . addressed to the general managers; letters relating to the customer's account at the head office, or containing instructions for the purchase or sale of securities should be addressed to the head office manager, while correspondence on the subject of bank shares should be conducted with the secretary.

With regard to correspondence through bankers for places abroad, London offices require their branches to communicate all such instructions to them, as far as possible, by Wednesday night's post for Eastern and South African mails; consequently the customer's instructions should be timed to reach the branch manager in conformity with the above arrangement. Mails for the United States are made up at least twice a week, the "fixed" days being Wednesdays and Saturdays; while those for South America are also very frequent.

SECTION II.

PASSPORTS, LETTERS OF CREDIT, CIRCULAR NOTES, FOREIGN AND COLONIAL DRAFTS, MAIL AND CABLE TRANSFERS.

It is well to remember, when about to travel abroad, that while in most foreign countries travellers are permitted to enter without passports, British subjects are nevertheless recommended to obtain them, as they are sometimes useful in supplying a ready means of identification. It is advisable not to delay the request to your banker until the last moment, as the Foreign Office requires one day's notice before issuing a passport, except in very urgent cases. Your bankers will readily give you all the information that is necessary with regard to obtaining passports, and will supply you with the necessary forms, transmitting your application to their London head office for lodgment with the Foreign Office. You will probably require to sign a certificate of recommendation and identity, which will be countersigned by your banker, recommending you and vouching for your British nationality. If a naturalised British subject, you will require to exhibit your certificate of naturalisation, and where surnames suggest foreign parentage the passport department nearly always requires p 'duction of a certificate of birth. Under ɔ circumstances will the passport departm nt issue a passport to an individual already abroaɑ. Such a person must apply at the nearest British legation or consulate. The passport requirements of foreign countries are very varied, and among them it may be noted that the Russian Consul-General in London requires an applicant for his "visa" to state his religion; and the rule is, not to append the "visa" until the applicant has signed his name at the foot of the passport. The authorities at the Imperial Ottoman Consulate always enquire at what port the applicant will enter the Turkish dominions. Special forms of application are required for children under 14 years of age.

With regard to circular letters of credit, you require to inform your banker, when making application, your full christian names, sending at the same time specimen signatures, and

stating for what length of time the credit is to
be available. As soon as these documents
come into your possession they should be
signed at the foot, for were they to get into
the hands of any dishonest person the credit
might very easily be drawn against.

For credits opened abroad the same particulars should be given as for circular letters.
Accredités drawing on London will usually
obtain a better rate of exchange than those
drawing on English provincial towns.

Should you have occasion to apply to your
banker for circular notes, you will require to
give your full christian names and to state
whether a letter of indication is required. It
is very important that the letter of indication
and the circular notes should be kept apart,
and that you should sign the letter of indication
as soon as you receive it.

When foreign and colonial drafts are required,
exact particulars should be given to your bank
manager as to the places on which drafts, etc.,
are to be drawn. Not only the name of the
town but also the state, and if possible the
county, where it is situated should be given.
If you can, you should supply a specimen of the
payee's signature, or, if this be impracticable,

a specimen of his handwriting. In America the responsibility of accounting to the proper party rests by law entirely on the paying banker; and if the payee be unable to identify himself, considerable inconvenience may be caused.

Where drafts or letters of credit are required on South Africa, Syria, Fiji, the Yukon District and certain places in South America, it is necessary to state whether the amount quoted is to be the net sum for which the draft is to be drawn—exchange and expenses being charged to the office applying,—or whether it is the *gross* sum available from which all charges are to be deducted before the issue of the draft.

As in the case of colonial drafts and letters of credit, so also when mail and cable transfers are required, it is necessary that full particulars should be supplied. The same may also be said as regards the observations respecting exchange and expenses. It is also to be noted that no foreign or colonial bank will effect a cable transfer, either for a customer or another bank, at their own risk. They generally require an indemnity guaranteeing them against any loss or damage that may arise in consequence of the message being incorrectly transmitted, delayed or misinterpreted, or through failure on the part of the paying bank to identify the payee. Should you, therefore, request your bank manager to instruct his London office to effect a cable transfer on your behalf, he will, in order to protect his own bank in regard to the indemnity which they will be giving, require an indemnity from you, —a request which is only fair and reasonable.

Periodical Payments Abroad.—Bankers are sometimes requested by their customers to arrange for the payment abroad,—weekly, monthly or otherwise—upon application, the applicants being usually of the class known as "remittance men." These transactions, however, do not greatly commend themselves either to the bankers on this side who receive the instructions, or to those to whom they are given; for they sometimes give opportunity to the entry of "undesirables" into the premises of banks situated in remote parts of the world. As a rule it may be taken that banks will only receive instructions of this nature when they are quite satisfied, both as to the source from which they emanate and the respectability of the applicant.

SECTION III.

RECLAIMING INCOME TAX.

ROUND about the month of April in each year, bankers are accustomed to receive requests from their shareholders for duplicate counterfoils of their dividend warrants, the originals having been lost or mislaid. These are required for the purpose of reclaiming income tax; and a few notes under this heading will probably be found of assistance.

In the first place, it should be noted that the request for such duplicate counterfoils should always be made by the person interested, and not through a third party. Of course, if it comes,—say from a firm of solicitors, or from some bank acting on behalf of the shareholders, well and good; but a bank will not readily give the required duplicate to some person or agency purporting to write on behalf of the shareholder until they receive the shareholder's authority. This rule will, no doubt, be found to obtain also as regards holdings in railway stocks, and in ordinary commercial or financial concerns. Perhaps it is scarcely necessary to add that a " second duplicate " cannot be furnished ; a banker, however, is sometimes asked for it.

A simple and useful plan for all who seek to recover income tax, is to put their vouchers in some large envelope as and when they receive the relative dividend warrants, placing with them the claim form which they receive every year, or third year, as the case may be, from the Inland Revenue. There will then be no difficulty in readily filling up and sending in the form and vouchers at the required time.

Another important item to note is the fact that in respect of stocks inscribed or registered at the Bank of England, income tax certificates are not required, except in the case of Indian Rupee Stocks. On your claim form you will find a special place set apart for such stocks. Certificates of deduction are also not necessary in respect of Government Life Annuity payments and Chancery Dividends.

Yet another point to be borne in mind is, that, when filling up your claim form, should you have any vouchers on which no deduction for income tax appears—that is to say, where the relative dividends are paid to you "free of income tax,"—you are entitled to treat such dividends as "net income," entering the amount of tax on the claim form as so much in the pound on the *gross* dividend. For example, if you receive a dividend of £95 free of income tax, such tax being at one shilling in the pound, the amount you are entitled to claim on is not £95, but £100, because you can consider the *gross* dividend as being £100, from which £5 tax has been deducted.

The filling in and lodgment of claims for customers does not in any way form part of a banker's duties, but a bank manager is always ready and willing to give advice and assistance in such matters to any of his customers who may need it, and the customer can, if he so desires, instruct the Inland Revenue authorities to remit the amount of tax claimed to his bankers for his account. Many people entrust this business to one or other of the various income tax recovery agents, who, for a consideration, readily undertake and carry it through on their behalf.

Possibly you do not receive your dividends direct, but save yourself the trouble and risk, in common with a very large number of bank

M

customers, by having your various dividends forwarded by the respective companies direct to your bankers for your credit. In such case the income tax vouchers will reach you with your paid cheques when your pass book is forwarded to you from time to time; and, as already hinted, it will probably save you considerable trouble, and it will certainly save others trouble also, if such vouchers are carefully preserved until they are required.

It is usually the first claim for income tax that will be most troublesome, for the novice will find that the Inland Revenue will insist, and rightly, upon having the claim form and vouchers in thorough order, and will require to be satisfied upon any point that is not clear. When, however, the first claim has been settled up, and the claimant has received his money order for the amount to be refunded, he will find, provided he has been careful to note the points at issue, that the preparation of subsequent claims is smooth sailing.

It may so happen that you are a beneficiary, jointly with others, in respect of certain stocks registered in the names of trustees. Where such is the case, and where dividends are paid to bankers who have, for example, to split up a single dividend on £1,000 Great Northern Railway 3 per cent. debenture stock equally between Mary Brown, Thomas Jones and Henry Robinson, the upper half of a dividend warrant will probably bear a rough note of such division made by the banker. Supposing you are one of the three, you can use the upper half of the warrant—that is to say, the income tax voucher—for reclaiming tax in respect of your own one-third ; and should either of the other beneficiaries need to make use of the same voucher for a similar purpose, it can be easily arranged with the Inland Revenue authorities.

Where stocks or shares have been purchased " cum dividend," but not in time for registration before the closing of the relative companies' books, a certificate of deduction of income tax will be given, if required, by the stock-brokers, since, in the circumstances above mentioned, the dividend will have to be claimed of the seller through the brokers.

Turning to the subject of coupons, income tax certificates are, of course, always readily obtainable in respect of these. Where coupons expressed in foreign currency (francs, marks, dollars, etc.) are sold or collected by bankers, income tax has to be deducted by them from the proceeds, and certificates of such deduction are always given when required by the customer.

As regards income tax on interest charged by banks on loans and overdrafts, the following extract from Dr. Heber Hart's valuable work, *The Law of Banking*, should be carefully noted. Bankers will, in such cases, give certificates that income tax has been, or will be, deducted from the profits of the bank.

"A banker must allow income tax to a customer upon interest accruing on a mortgage debt. But interest upon a loan by a banker to a customer for a period of less than a year is not within the words 'any yearly interest of money or any annuity or other annual payment' in 16 & 17 Vict. c. 34, s. 40, and therefore the customer is not entitled to deduct income tax from such interest.

"'In point of business,' said Lindley, L.J., 'a mortgage is not a short loan; but a banker's loan at three months is a totally different thing. That is a short loan, it is intended and understood to be a short loan, and the difference in practice between the two is perfectly well known to every business man.'"

SECTION IV.

CHANGE OF ADDRESS.

It is remarkable to note the variety of wrong methods that are adopted for giving notice of change of address. Some there are who send no notice at all, but allow dividend warrants, pass books, or what not to take their chance of finding them, and subsequently write in an aggrieved tone at their non-receipt. Others get someone to write on their behalf, forgetting that such a course might easily lead to fraud, or forgery, or other difficulty, if the bank were to accept such instructions. Perhaps a still more common error is to send a printed notice without a written signature; this, of course, does not constitute a valid authority for the required change. Yet a fourth style that is adopted is that of writing in the third person; such a notification, however, the bank will ordinarily accept, provided that they can find that it is in the handwriting of the person whose address it is desired to alter and from whom it purports to come.

Having thus shown how *not* to notify your change of address, the simple points to observe are :—

(1) That your letter should be headed with the subject matter, *e.g.*, bank shares, current account, deposit account, the name of registered stocks or shares, etc., in respect of which you desire your address to be altered..

(2) That it should notify your removal from _____to_____, and

(3) That it should bear your signature.

If the notification has reference to more than one matter, the letter should mention each subject or department to which it relates. For instance, a person holding Consols, New Zealand 4 per cent. stock and Transvaal 3 per cent. stock would require to mention each of these accounts to the Bank of England, otherwise his address might be altered in only one of them. A case occurred within the writer's knowledge where a lady, who was frequently changing her address, notified a bank as to her removal, but omitted to state to what matter her communication had reference. She was a holder of shares in the bank, and the register was altered accordingly, the clerk, into whose hands the letter came, doubtless thinking that the matter was thus completed. But she also held certain stock, the books of which were kept at the same bank; the letter did not pass on to the clerk in charge; the dividend consequently went to some boarding-house at which the lady had previously resided, and it was stolen and cashed.

In a great number of instances those who have stocks or shares registered in their name give instructions to the company or agent by whom the dividends are paid to forward dividends to their bankers. In such cases, it is always well to bear in mind to notify the company or agent of your change of address, otherwise circulars, notices, and possibly still more important documents, such as offers of allotment, etc., may fail to reach you.

Frequently, after a bank has issued its half-yearly dividends, it receives a number of acknowledgments from shareholders who state that they have changed their address, but that the dividend has been sent on to them. Many, however, merely mention their change of address (of which the arrival of the dividend has reminded them), but omit to mention at the same time that the dividend has safely reached them. This item, however, should not be omitted, as the bank may otherwise be left in doubt as to whether the dividend has been sent on from the former address or not. Probably, on the counterfoils of most bank share dividend warrants, a request will be found that any change of address should be at once notified to the secretary ; this simple rule, if followed—as it is in the majority of cases,— would save much trouble to all concerned. It happens, however, over and over again, that through a shareholder's omission to notify his banker of his change of address, the warrant is returned through the post, and the banker therefore can only hold it until he hears from the shareholder. Or it may be that the shareholder has died, and the banker therefore retains the warrant, upon its return through the post office, until proof of death is lodged with him and the warrant has been claimed ; taking care, of course, should another dividend become due before death has been proved, that *that* dividend also is retained.

What has been said under this heading with regard to change of address in respect of holders of bank shares applies, of course, equally to the shares or stocks in other companies, corporations, or any other concern.

SECTION V.

POWERS OF ATTORNEY (GENERAL).

IT has already been remarked in the chapter on Bank of England regulations that that bank will not accept general powers of attorney where sale or transfer of stocks inscribed with them is concerned. If, therefore, anyone by reason of his going abroad, or from other circumstances, contemplates giving a power to someone who shall act on his behalf during his absence, or on account of illness, or from other causes, the above regulation should be borne in mind, so far as such stocks are concerned.

General powers of attorney, however, are of course required at various times and under a variety of conditions. Should you, for any reason, need to give such a power, you would be wise to entrust the matter to a solicitor rather than attempt to make out such a document yourself, or even to copy some similar document which you may have access

to. All the details to which the power is
intended to apply should be furnished to the
solicitor; and, for your guidance, it would be
well to note the following points :—

(1) It is frequently desirable to limit the
period for which the power shall be
available, and you should, therefore, tell
your legal adviser if you desire that
it should only remain in force, say for
one or two years, or until some specified date.

(2) Do not forget that under *no* circumstances
can a trustee delegate his authority.
This is a point that is sometimes overlooked or ignored, and powers of
attorney are produced to bankers for
the purpose of registration, say in
respect of certain stock standing in the
name of the person who gives the
power, expressly disclosing therein the
fact that such stock is a trustee holding.
The bank has no option in such cases
but to refuse the power, and has
probably to put up with disagreeable
remarks or correspondence in consequence, whereas the fault lies entirely
with those who framed the power.

Moreover, it is equally useless to hedge the matter round by making use of such a phrase as "So far as I can lawfully delegate my authority as trustee, etc.," for the authority cannot be lawfully delegated.

(3) Be as definite as possible, but at the same time do not omit to have the general and inclusive clauses embodied in the power, as a banker is sometimes able to fall back upon these where there is lack of completeness or definiteness in the instructions which were intended to apply to him.

One point worth mentioning here, as one that is frequently overlooked, is the advisability of including a clause, giving the attorney power either to "accept" or "renounce" the offer of allotment in any new issue that may be made in respect of stocks or shares held. The inclusion of such a clause would frequently save considerable trouble.

(4) If no time limit is stated in the power of attorney, remember to advise every person, firm, or company with whom it has been registered when, from any cause, it becomes obsolete.

(5) Bear in mind, that, should you at any.
time execute transfers, sign dividend
warrants, or personally do any of the
acts for which you gave the power,
when such power has been registered
with various companies, the power
ceases to be in force. To obviate this,
the person who gave the power will
sometimes have a clause included therein to the following effect :—

" And notwithstanding that I may at
any time subsequent to the date of this
power personally carry out any of the
acts, deeds, and transactions for the
purposes of which this power has been
given, this power shall continue a
subsisting power and remain in force
until the revocation thereof by me in
writing."

(6) When some considerable time has
elapsed from the date of the execution
of the power, and its registration
with any bank or company, inquiry
will probably be made, now and again,
as to whether it still remains in force :
this is, of course, but natural and
reasonable.

Generally, it should be added that powers of attorney are sometimes sent to bankers with the express statement that they are to be registered with a view to the selling of shares and receipt of dividends, whereas no such powers are conferred by the document, and even the "elastic" clauses will not permit of such an interpretation. It might, therefore, be repeated, that the more simply and definitely powers of attorney are drawn up, the better it will be for all concerned. In fact, where possible, it would be advisable for you to see your banker before you have your power of attorney drafted; but if this be impracticable it would, at least, be well for you, before going abroad, to be satisfied that you have not left behind you a document which is useless for the purposes for which you intended it.

SECTION VI.

INDEMNITIES.

THE necessity for an indemnity from a banker often arises, the causes being very varied. Goods are immediately required but the relative bill of lading has not yet arrived; a coupon has been lost; bank note burned; share certificate cannot be found; allotment letter inadvertently destroyed; these are but specimens of accidents that are frequently taking place. In almost all instances the bank or company requiring the indemnity will only accept such a document from a banker, the latter, in turn, usually taking a "back" indemnity from his customer. Probably there is no bank having a large number of shareholders which does not receive a few letters each half-year from some of them, stating that they have not received their dividend warrants. This is especially the case in the summer months, when some shareholders omit to notify the bank of their absence from home. In the majority of cases, however, it generally transpires, upon the shareholder receiving a courteous acknowledgment of his letter from the banker requesting him to make further search, and to repeat his application for a duplicate warrant in the course of a month or two, that the original warrant comes to light.

As regards missing share certificates, it does not always follow that a company will issue a duplicate merely against an indemnity. There are cases when such an indemnity will only be accepted if given by a guarantee society, and such society would naturally make a charge, probably of a percentage on the market value of the security in respect of which the indemnity is given.

LIFE ANNUITIES, PENSIONS, AND CHANCERY DIVIDENDS.

WHERE it is desired to purchase a life annuity and to receive the payments as they become due, your banker can readily arrange matters for you. In giving the order for purchase, the banker is required to state, either the amount of the annuity required to be bought, or the amount of money to be invested in purchase of the annuity; together with the full name, address and description of the annuitant, and age next birthday. In addition to these particulars others may be required; but all necessary forms in connection therewith will be sent you by your banker. As is well known, an annuity has not necessarily to be taken out on the life of the intending purchaser, but can be obtained on the life of anyone whom the purchaser may name, provided the purchase is made for the sole use and benefit of that person.

Annuity payments become due quarterly, *viz.*, 5th January, April, July, and October. Income tax is recoverable in much the same way as in the case of Government stocks inscribed at the Bank of England, that is to say, no voucher need accompany the claim form.

India Pensions.—If you require your banker to collect your pension for you, you must furnish him with the following particulars :—

(1) The full name, rank, and present address of the person entitled to the pension.

(2) The amount of the pension and the fund from which it is derived.

(3) The dates on which the pension payments are due.

Home Service Pensions.—In cases where a banker is required to collect these, a letter must be addressed by the beneficiary to the Paymaster-General stating the name of the bankers who will receive payment on his behalf. Full particulars of the pension, as in the case of India pensions above referred to, should be given to the bankers.

Chancery Dividends.—These are collected by bankers for their customers upon the execution,

N

by the latter, of special request forms (free of stamp duty), supplied for the purpose. A certificate or affidavit to the effect that the beneficiary is alive on, or subsequent to, the date when the dividend becomes due, has always to be made ; except, of course, where it is a corporate body, such as the Mayor and Aldermen, for the time being, of Blanktown.

As in the case of Government stocks inscribed at the Bank of England, no certificate of deduction will be necessary when making a claim for return of income tax.

INDEX.

'ND DUNC'

Printed in the United States
101124LV00002B/268/A

9 781406 739480